THE LITTLE BOOK OF CRICKET

WORLD CUP SPECIAL EDITION

Written by Ralph Dellor and Stephen Lamb

THE LITTLE BOOK OF
CRICKET

This edition first published in the UK in 2006
By Green Umbrella

© Green Umbrella Publishing 2006

www.greenumbrella.co.uk

Publishers Jules Gammond & Vanessa Gardner

All rights reserved. No part of this work may be reproduced or utilised in any form or by any means, electronic or mechanical, including photocopying, recording or by any information storage and retrieval system, without prior written permission of the publisher.

Printed and bound in China

ISBN-13: 978-1-905828-04-3
ISBN-10: 1-905828-04-7

The views in this book are those of the author but they are general views only and readers are urged to consult the relevant and qualified specialist for individual advice in particular situations.

Green Umbrella Publishing hereby exclude all liability to the extent permitted by law of any errors or omissions in this book and for any loss, damage or expense (whether direct or indirect) suffered by a third party relying on any information contained in this book.

All our best endeavours have been made to secure copyright clearance for every photograph used but in the event of any copyright owner being overlooked please address correspondence to Green Umbrella Publishing.
www.greenumbrella.co.uk

Contents

4   The World Cup

24   Origins & Development

46   Test Cricket

110   The Players

Chapter 1

The World Cup

RIGHT Keith Fletcher batting for England against India at Lord's in the first World Cup match of 1975

WHEN ENGLAND WERE ON TOUR in Australia in 1970/71, the third Test of a six-match series was scheduled for Melbourne over the New Year holiday. Because of persistent and heavy rain there was no play on the first three days, and the match was abandoned. Instead there was a limited-overs game played on what was scheduled to be the final day of the Test as a gesture to ticket-holders.

Thus January 5th 1971 took its place in cricket history as the day on which the first one-day international was played. It was 40 overs a side, at the same venue that had seen the birth of Test cricket 94 years earlier. It was between the same two sides and had the same result, an Australian victory. Some 46,000 spectators turned up, and handed over considerable amounts of money to witness what was to prove the start of a new era in international cricket.

The following year, one-day internationals became an important feature of the fixture list and, once their popularity had become evident, it was only a matter of time before the nations came together to play a world cup competition. That time was destined to be 1975, with England the venue.

To justify the event's billing as a World Cup without the banned South Africans, it was felt that there should be wider representation than the six Test countries that were established at the time. A rather damp and squelchy qualifying competition was held resulting in Sri Lanka and East Africa joining the six Test nations in two groups of four. If the tournament itself was to be a success, it needed fair weather, even though three days had been set aside for each of the 15 scheduled matches. By the time it got under way a hot dry spell had begun, and not a single minute was lost to the weather throughout the entire tournament.

Not that Sunil Gavaskar could claim sunstroke in the first match. Some 20,000 spectators were at Lord's to watch England play India, and they enjoyed seeing the hosts run up a total of 334 for four in their 60 overs. Could India's stroke makers like Farokh Engineer and Gundappa Viswanath challenge such a total? Nobody will ever know, because Gavaskar decided it was too great a challenge and opted for batting practice. He hit one boundary from the 174 balls he faced, to finish 36 not out in a total of 132 for three. England won by 202 runs.

Headingley was full for the first time in nearly a decade as Australia beat Pakistan. The West Indies emerged as the favourites, with some powerful displays in a form of the game tailor-made to show off their characteristic strengths, although they survived a thriller at Edgbaston to beat Pakistan by a single wicket. The meeting of Australia and West Indies at the Oval

THE LITTLE BOOK OF CRICKET 5

THE WORLD CUP

ABOVE Prince Philip looks on as West Indies captain Clive Lloyd raises the World Cup after beating Australia in 1975

Headingley ground where a green, used pitch and humid, overcast conditions caused the ball to swing and seam prodigiously. Australia's Ian Chappell put England in and Gary Gilmour bowled them out. At one time 37 for seven, England made a partial recovery to 93 all out. Australia, at 39 for six, were also struggling, but Gilmour wielded his bat effectively for 28 not out from as many balls and Australia got home by four wickets.

In the other semi-final at the Oval, New Zealand reached 98 for one before suffering a spectacular collapse to be all out for 158. West Indies were 133 for one before a mini-collapse narrowed the margin of victory to five wickets. The public were enthralled by the competition, and interest in the final was widespread despite the absence of the home side. If England were not in the Lord's final, Australia v West Indies would do very nicely instead.

was the highlight of the group matches, with West Indies winning by seven wickets to establish a semi-final line-up of England against Australia, and West Indies versus New Zealand.

The 'Ashes' semi was played on a

THE WORLD CUP

Australia won the toss and fielded with immediate results. Dennis Lillee induced the feisty little left-hander, Roy Fredericks, to tread on his wicket as he hooked him for six. Gilmour and Jeff Thomson each took a wicket to reduce West Indies to 50 for three in the 19th over. Then Clive Lloyd joined Rohan Kanhai to add 149 in 26 overs. Lloyd's hundred came from a mere 82 balls (the second 50 from 30 balls) and his side were in a strong position with 291 on the board.

Australia went after the target with a purpose, but their progress was hindered by no fewer than five run outs, the result of some indifferent running and outstanding fielding, especially from Viv Richards who claimed three on his own. Australia were facing defeat on 233 for nine when the unlikely batting partnership of Lillee and Thomson took them to within 18 runs of a win, before Thomson became the final run-out victim.

World Cup cricket was established as a massive triumph, well supported throughout and entertaining right up to the last ball. The final had been played on the longest day of the year, and needed to be with the match starting at 11am and going on for nearly ten hours. It was for that reason, to say nothing of the fine weather, good organisation and crowd support, that the ICC decided that the tournament should return to England

ABOVE West Indian batsman Collis King scored a match-turning 86 against England in the final of 1979

THE LITTLE BOOK OF CRICKET 7

THE WORLD CUP

RIGHT David Gower on his way to a century against Sri Lanka in a World Cup match at Taunton in 1983

four years later. So in 1979 the world's cricket stars gathered there again. To determine which Associate Members would join the competition proper, another qualifying tournament was held, but this time with its own raison d'etre. The two finalists in the ICC Trophy, as it was termed, would go through. They were Sri Lanka, who took the trophy, and Canada.

Sri Lanka went on to win their group match against India, causing a major upset. With their match against West Indies rained off, they took six points to finish above India in their group, from which West Indies and New Zealand went through to the semi-finals. From the other group it was England and Pakistan, while Australia, without their World Series stars, were eliminated along with Canada.

The semi-final at Old Trafford was a thriller, resulting in an England win by just nine runs as New Zealand mounted stronger opposition than might have been expected. Meanwhile at the Oval, West Indies and Pakistan produced a batting exhibition on a pitch prepared for such an occasion. The West Indies scored 293 for six before Pakistan's batsmen made a brave but unavailing attempt to beat the holders.

When West Indies stumbled at the start of the final, a competitive match

THE WORLD CUP

was anticipated. But Richards, with a superb 138 not out, and Collis King dismissed any such notion as they bludgeoned England's under-strength bowling attack. Chasing 287 to win, the hosts made a solid start, reaching 129 before the first wicket fell, but they were always behind the required rate and were left needing 158 from the last 22 overs against an inspired Joel Garner, who took five for four inside two overs. West Indies retained the Cup, as did England in a way, for the ICC decided that the competition should return there in four years' time.

In 1983, the West Indies were still ruling the cricketing roost. But this was to be the tournament of the upset, starting in the early matches and going through to the final itself. It was also the first time matches were played away from the major Test grounds. This was necessitated by the decision to have two group matches against each of the other sides, so that the tournament as a whole consisted of

THE WORLD CUP

27 matches rather than 15. So Bristol, Chelmsford, Derby, Leicester, Southampton, Swansea, Taunton, Tunbridge Wells and Worcester all became international venues.

The first upset occurred at Trent Bridge where Zimbabwe, who qualified from the ICC Trophy, beat the mighty Australians. Australia put them in to bat, no doubt anticipating a quick dismissal, scoring the required runs and moving on to Leeds for their next match against the West Indies. Thanks to 69 from their captain Duncan Fletcher, who was later to become England coach, Zimbabwe reached 239 for six. Fletcher then took 4 for 42 from 11 overs, and Australia were beaten by 13 runs.

In the return match at Southampton, a late collapse saw Zimbabwe fall short of their previous success by 32 runs, but they seemed set to upset India at Tunbridge Wells. India were 17 for five before they began their recovery. Even so, their eighth wicket fell with only 140 on the board. They did not lose another, as Kapil Dev played one of the most explosive innings in cricket history. He hit 16 fours and six sixes while scoring

THE WORLD CUP

175 not out from a mere 138 balls to produce a bizarrely uneven scorecard for India's total of 266. The next highest score was 24 not out from Syed Kirmani. Zimbabwe lost by 31 runs.

With Australia winning only one other match, thrashing India, who in turn beat the West Indies, it was West Indies and India who went through to the semi-finals from that group. Sri Lanka managed one win against New Zealand in the other, meaning that England and Pakistan went forward, although Pakistan only did so by virtue of a better run rate at the expense of New Zealand. The margin was 0.08 of a run per over.

In England's semi-final against India at Old Trafford, none of their batsmen went on after making a start and they were bowled out for 213. India won by six wickets. Pakistan's batsmen suffered a similar fate to England's at the Oval against the West Indies, who strode into the final by eight wickets, knocking off the 185 needed to win in 48.4 overs.

After bowling India out in the final, West Indies needed only 184 to win. Their pace machine had prevailed and it was thought to be a mere formality for one of the most powerful batting line-ups in world cricket to knock off the runs. How could Greenidge and Haynes, Lloyd and Richards fail? The

LEFT Kapil Dev of India on his way to 175 not out against Zimbabwe in 1983

BELOW Indian supporters are euphoric after India beat the West Indies in the 1983 final

ABOVE A jubilant Simon O'Donnell of Australia takes a wicket during the final in Calcutta, 1987

answer was that the Indian peashooters might not have the firepower of the Caribbean cannons, but were ridiculously successful. The gentle medium pace of Mohinder Amarnath, Madan Lal and Roger Binny ripped the heart out of the West Indies to leave them 43 runs short of their target. The whole Indian Diaspora went berserk with happiness, while the result had breathed new life into the World Cup.

As a consequence of India's historic win at Lord's, the World Cup of 1987 left England for the first time. Despite the diplomatic standoff between India and Pakistan at governmental level, cricket transcended such problems as the two countries successfully staged the tournament between them. No

THE WORLD CUP

fewer than 21 venues were used in a tournament spread over six weeks to allow for the distances to be travelled, but it was still a success.

The tone was set in the group matches, with Australia beating India in Madras by a single run, and then New Zealand at Indore by three runs. New Zealand themselves beat Zimbabwe by an identical margin, and England took 35 off the last three overs to beat West Indies by two wickets, while Pakistan beat West Indies by one wicket.

Everything was designed to produce the final that would have satisfied the vast audiences in India and Pakistan, but it was not to be. Graham Gooch quite literally swept England into the final with 115 in Bombay, as the Indian spinners were rendered impotent. Meanwhile in Lahore, Pakistan fell to Australia's Craig McDermott who took five wickets in his team's 18-run win.

There would be a new name on the new trophy, as both England and Australia had fallen to the West Indies in previous finals. Eden Gardens in Calcutta provided a frenzied backdrop as Australia made 253 for five, but England were soon on course to break the record for a World Cup final chase. Australian captain Allan Border might have run out of ideas when he brought himself on to bowl to his opposite number Mike Gatting, on 41 at the time. Gatting went for a reverse sweep from the first ball he faced from Border and gave a catch to wicket-keeper Greg Dyer. Allan Lamb took up the challenge with some lusty accumulation, but despite a late flurry from Philip DeFreitas, England fell seven runs short.

The 1992 tournament was played in Australia and New Zealand, and yet again England reached the final and lost. The format was changed from two qualifying groups producing the semi-finalists to one group of nine teams playing one match against the other eight, with the

BELOW The participating countries line up in the opening ceremony before the 1992 World Cup in Australia and New Zealand

THE WORLD CUP

top four going into the semi-finals. That meant 39 matches were played, 14 of them in New Zealand. With so much travelling involved, there was no possibility of rain days, and the regulation for achieving results in such games was to cause all sorts of problems as the tournament unfolded. It included the South Africans for the first time, re-admitted to the international fold.

South Africa featured prominently in the bizarre rain rules. In a group match against them, England lost nine overs due to a weather interruption, but the target was reduced by just 11 runs and England scraped home. Then England bowled out Pakistan for 74 and were 24 for one after eight overs when the rain forced a no result. The point thus gained by Pakistan was enough to put them into the semi-finals at the expense of Australia and the West Indies. England were there as well, despite losing embarrassingly to Zimbabwe, along with New Zealand and South Africa.

In the semi-final in Auckland, New Zealand held the upper hand for a long time, but Pakistan edged home by four wickets thanks to Javed

THE WORLD CUP

Miandad. Meanwhile in Sydney, England scored 252 for six against South Africa, who needed 22 to win from 13 balls when the rain came. This was re-assessed to be 22 from seven balls when the rain stopped, but when the teams came back on the field, the scoreboard suddenly showed that 21 were needed from just one ball. England would probably have won anyway, but there were hoots of derision from a crowd robbed of a potentially exciting finish.

Pakistan scored a respectable 249 for six in the final, staged in Melbourne. England were moving closer to the target when there was a drinks break and captain Imran Khan exhorted his play-

LEFT Imran Khan, the captain of Pakistan, displays the World Cup in Melbourne, 1992

BELOW Armed guards mingle with the Sri Lankans during the presentations after the abandonment of the semi-final at Eden Gardens in 1996

THE LITTLE BOOK OF CRICKET 15

ABOVE Riot police surround the boundary after the abandonment of the 1996 semi-final between India and Sri Lanka

ers to imitate the action of the cornered tiger. Directly afterwards, Wasim Akram earned his stripes by bowling both Allan Lamb and Chris Lewis, to set up Imran himself to take a wicket with his last ball in international cricket and lift the cup.

After the dual hosting arrangements of 1992, there was a tripartite agreement in 1996 featuring India, Pakistan and Sri Lanka. Of these, either India or Pakistan might have been fancied to become the first host nation to win the cup, but there was a delightful surprise in store. Australia and West Indies refused to go to Sri Lanka because of civil strife, but it scarcely affected their chances of progressing because three minnows had been included. West Indies lost to Kenya in one of the greatest upsets of all time, but with the Kenyans, along with Holland and United Arab Emirates eliminated with Zimbabwe, the newly introduced quarter-final stage included all the major countries.

Sri Lanka had developed a new approach to the limited-overs game. Rather than waiting for the final ten overs for an all-out assault, Sanath Jayasuriya and Romesh Kaluwitharana blitzed the attack for the first 15 overs while there

THE WORLD CUP

were fielding restrictions. England fell foul of them in the quarter-finals, while India beat Pakistan, West Indies defeated the fancied South Africans and Australia accounted for New Zealand.

Australia overcame the West Indies by five runs in one semi-final in Chandigarh as the men from the Caribbean lost their last eight wickets for 37 runs. If that was dramatic, it was nothing compared with the other one in Calcutta where Sri Lanka made 251 for eight before India collapsed to 120 for eight in 34.1 overs. It caused an explosion of unrest in the stands and the match was called off, forfeited by India.

So to the final in Lahore, the first day/night international to be held in Pakistan. Arjuna Ranatunga won the toss and took the unusual step of putting Australia in to bat in order to avoid fielding in the heavy dew that fell locally. Australia slumped from 137 for one to 241 for seven, before Aravinda de Silva, with 107 not out, and the captain steered their side to a four-wicket win with 22 balls to spare. The scenes of jubilation from Colombo to Kandy lifted the spirits of an entire, war-torn nation.

In 1999 the World Cup returned to England, although it has to be said that the spectacular opening ceremonies that characterise modern sporting events were notably absent. A few fireworks left a pall of smoke across Lord's, making the rest of the ceremony practically invisible, a world cup Song that failed to mention cricket at all that was not released until after England had been eliminated, and the poor performance of the home team completed an unenthralling competition.

There were, nonetheless, good matches and some exciting cricket. England started impressively enough, beating the holders by eight wickets at Lord's. However, they were to lose out on net run-rate to Zimbabwe and India, with South Africa joining the other two from Group A in the 'Super Six' stage. Pakistan finished top of Group B, despite a highly suspicious defeat by

BELOW Fireworks at the opening ceremony of the 1999 World Cup at the Lord's

THE WORLD CUP

Bangladesh in a match that had no bearing on later rounds. Australia and New Zealand joined them in the next stage.

Points and net run-rate from matches against other Super Six qualifiers were carried forward, resulting in Pakistan starting on top of the new round-robin table and Australia bottom. The matches resulted in Pakistan staying top, Australia moving up to second, with South Africa and New Zealand completing the semi-final line up. Pakistan easily overcame New Zealand by nine wickets at Old Trafford, while the high drama was reserved for Edgbaston where Australia met South Africa.

Australia were bowled out for 213. Lance Klusener then took South Africa to the brink with 31 from 14 balls, including consecutive fours off Damien Fleming to bring the scores level. Just one run was required from four balls with Klusener on strike. Allan Donald should have been run out for backing up too far, but the throw to the non-striker's end missed. Klusener drove the next ball and ran; Donald dropped his bat having previously made his ground knowing there

THE WORLD CUP

LEFT Jubilation on the Australian balcony after victory over Pakistan in the World Cup final of 1999

were still two balls to come. The Australians relayed the ball to Adam Gilchrist who removed the bails with Donald, this time, well short. With the match ending sensationally in a tie, Australia went through by virtue of a net run-rate superior to South Africa in the Super Six stage. In keeping with the organisation and presentation of the tournament, few spectators on the ground had the slightest idea that Australia had qualified for the final against Pakistan.

If the pyrotechnics of the opening at Lord's had left a lot to be desired, the final on the same ground turned out to be a damp squib as a spectacle. After the tense finish at Edgbaston, Australia cruised past Pakistan to take the trophy while hardly breaking sweat. Pakistan made 132 and Australia got them for two wickets in a match lasting a total of 59.1 overs. End of story.

It was thought that South Africa, so cruelly excluded from the final in 1999, to say nothing of 1992, would be in their element in the 2003 competition, which was played in southern Africa. Matches were staged in Kenya and Zimbabwe as well as in the Republic,

THE WORLD CUP

ABOVE Preparation for the 2003 World Cup at Newlands, Cape Town

which, in itself, gave the tournament political intrigue, as both New Zealand and England refused to play in those countries on security grounds. Wins were awarded to the home sides, so Zimbabwe joined Australia and India in the Super Six from Group A, while Kenya were the unlikely qualifiers from Group B, along with Sri Lanka and New Zealand.

Sides like Bangladesh, Namibia, Canada and Holland expected elimination at that stage. Less so England and Pakistan from Group A, along with South Africa and West Indies from Group B. Just as at Edgbaston in 1999, South Africa's dismissal had a touch of farce and tragedy about it. At

Durban against Sri Lanka in their last qualifying match, thickening drizzle made it inevitable that the Duckworth/Lewis method would decide the result. Messages were sent out to the batsmen in the middle, and the scoreboard showed the figure 229. Mark Boucher hoisted a six to reach that total and thought he had won the match, so defended the last ball. In fact, he had only brought the scores level; 230 was the required total.

Because of the political machinations of games forfeited, Kenya, who also beat Sri Lanka, started the Super Six in second place behind Australia. When they beat their fellow beneficiaries of the boycott, Zimbabwe, they found themselves in the semi-finals along with India, Sri Lanka and Australia, looking unbeatable even without Shane Warne who had failed a drug test. So it was to prove.

Australia made heavy weather of the semi-final against Sri Lanka. They scored just 212 for seven, partly due to the fact that Adam Gilchrist walked after edging a sweep on to his pad to be caught. Meanwhile India were far too professional for Kenya whose dream-like journey through the tournament came to an abrupt awakening. Almost as abrupt as India's experience in the final as Ricky Ponting's 140 not out powered Australia to 359 for two. India fell 125 runs short.

ABOVE Mark Boucher hits out during the opening match of the 2003 tournament between South Africa and the West Indies.

THE LITTLE BOOK OF CRICKET 21

ABOVE Adam Gilchrist, captain Ricky Ponting and Damien Martyn lift the World Cup for Australia in 2003

RIGHT The World Cup Trophy for the 1999 tournament

Such was the success of World Cup cricket that the authorities opted to stage another competition in between the main tournaments, which nowadays goes under the name of the ICC Champions Trophy. Usually referred to as a mini-world cup, its purpose is to raise money for the development of cricket in areas where the game is growing. While it is a tournament countries try to win, they frequently send understrength sides to take part as other events take precedence, and the results seldom make an impact in the greater scheme of things.

The same can be said of the proliferation of one-day tournaments around the world. Triangular and even quadrangular events abound, with Sharjah earning a reputation for putting on more one-day internationals than any other ground, and also staging four Test matches when the security situation in Pakistan prevented other teams from travelling there. Its connection with illegal gambling activities has long been suspected but never proven.

In general, one-day internationals are reliable sources of revenue for all countries. World Cup tournaments are different, but so many inferior

THE WORLD CUP

competitions are now played around the globe that there is a real danger of saturation. But every now and then there is one that makes for compulsive viewing. One such took place in March 2006 at the Wanderers Stadium in Johannesburg. Australia scored an incredible world record 434 for four in their 50 overs to make the game absolutely safe. Safe, that was, until South Africa scored 438 for nine off 49.5 overs! International one-day cricket has come a long way from that day in Melbourne back in 1971.

There have been suggestions for a World Cup of Test cricket, but the practicalities of such a notion have prevented it from coming to fruition. That is not the case with Twenty20 cricket. The impact of this form of the game, first in England and then in other parts of the world, has made a Twenty20 World Cup inevitable. The ICC took only a short time to appreciate the potential of a tournament of this nature and so scheduled the inaugural competition for South Africa in 2007. With the World Cup itself taking place in the Caribbean earlier the same year, the international calendar becomes ever more crowded.

Chapter 2

Origins & Development

THEORIES ABOUND ABOUT THE origins of cricket. There are numerous references to bat and ball games being played in ancient times in England, across Europe and even claims that it all began in China. However, it is generally accepted that the modern game originated in the Weald of southeast England, played by shepherds as a means of whiling away the time spent watching their flocks on those upland pastures.

No doubt sheep grazed the grass short enough to accommodate the early practice of rolling the ball along the ground. It is quite conceivable that a shepherd's crook would have been used as the bat, hence the curved shape of the earliest examples. The very name of cricket is thought to come from the Anglo-Saxon word *cricce*, meaning a stick.

There were the means at hand to construct a ball. Matted wool could be fashioned into some sort of serviceable shape, with wax from the raddle (fitted to rams to check when a ewe had been tupped) to hold it together. But what of the target at which such a ball was propelled? Again, the entrance to a sheepfold, or wicket gate (perhaps deriving from wicker gate), was to hand and would serve the purpose admirably.

Just as the format of the modern game can be traced from these rustic beginnings, so may the implements

ORIGINS & DEVELOPMENT

ABOVE A game of cricket being played on the Artillery Ground in London, 1743

have evolved from rudimentary balls and sticks to those of the present day. The early balls, of wool, wound cloth or even chunks of wood, became more uniformly spherical in shape. Later, cork or some other form of stuffing was used to form the ball's centre, while a covering of leather was stitched around it. That was the prototype for today's ball.

Regulations concerning size and weight followed. In the first attempt to codify the Laws of Cricket, in 1744, the only thing that mattered about the ball was its weight, which could be no less than five ounces and no more than six. 30 years later this was narrowed down to between

ORIGINS & DEVELOPMENT

ABOVE Portrait of a boy holding a cricket bat by Francis Cotes (1726-1770)

specifying that it should be between nine and nine and a quarter inches. In 1927 this was reduced to the present-day figure, no less than eight and thirteen sixteenths of an inch (22.4 centimetres), and no greater than nine inches (22.9 cm). The ball used in women's cricket is slightly smaller and lighter, while for juniors it is still more so (four and three-quarter ounces).

But how did the bat develop from a mere stick off a tree, or shepherd's crook? These were honed into a club, which itself evolved into something like a present-day hockey stick. This shape, with a distinctive curve at the bottom, was designed to deal with the underarm deliveries of earlier days. These were propelled all along the ground in a literal derivation of the original "bowling". The first signs of a shoulder emerged, and the now customary splice followed so that, once the foot of the blade had lost its curve, the bat had virtually become what we see today.

The development of equipment reflects how the game has evolved since its formative years. One of the very first illustrations thought to depict cricket appeared in Bede's Life of St. Cuthbert. Dated between 1120 and 1130, the pic-

five and a half ounces, or 155.9 grams, and five and three-quarter ounces (163g).

It was not until 1838 that a ruling was made about the ball's circumference,

ABOVE Cricket being played at White Conduit House, Islington, the original home of the MCC

ture shows a montage of several figures involved in sporting activity, including one wielding what could have been an early cricket bat. The accompanying text describes "The boy St. Cuthbert, too fond of playing games". The fact that the manuscript originated in Durham shows how soon the game may have spread from south-east England.

Moving on to 1300, an entry in the Wardrobe Accounts of Edward I is thought to refer to cricket. It is for a sum paid to Master John de Leek, the chaplain to Prince Edward, the King's son, "for monies paid out himself or by the hands of others, for the said Prince playing at creag and other sports at Westminster on 10th March, 100 shillings." The word creag has not been found anywhere else to disprove the theory that the young prince was playing an early form of cricket.

To illustrate how widespread cricket was becoming, there was a reference to a game involving a bat and a ball in a village in northern France in 1478. At that time, the region was under strong English influence, but the manuscript refers to "criquet" which, in old French, meant a post or even wicket. There is also evidence of a game resembling cricket being played in medieval France,

ORIGINS & DEVELOPMENT

ABOVE A lady cricketer taking a catch, 1889

with an illustration of a batsman defending a tree stump with fielders ranged all around.

The first reference to cricket by name comes in 1598, when a court case in Guildford adjudicated on disputed land. A witness, by then 59 years of age, mentions when, "being a scholar of the Free School of Guildford, he and diverse of his fellows did runne and play there at creckett and other plaies". Such testimony affirms that when the witness, a John Derrick, had been a scholar (around 1550), cricket was known by name.

ORIGINS & DEVELOPMENT

Also at the end of the 16th century, an Italian-English dictionary translated the word "sgrittare" as "to play cricket-a-wicket and be merry". A French dictionary translated the word "crosse" as "the crooked staff wherewith boys play at cricket", and when that renowned Puritan, Oliver Cromwell, arrived in London as an 18-year-old in 1617, it was reported that he "gained himself the name of royster" by playing, among other sports and pastimes, cricket. By 1656, Cromwell's men had banned the game in Ireland where there was an edict ordering all "sticks and balls" to be burnt.

Many of these early references seem to confine cricket to being a children's activity, but it was not long before evidence surfaces of the game being played by adults as well. Near Chichester, a case was brought against six men for playing cricket when they should have been at Sunday evensong. Furthermore, two churchwardens were named and shamed for aiding and abetting them.

Well before the popularity of the Sunday League, cricket was coming into conflict with the church. In 1629 a case was brought against Henry Cuffin, a curate on Romney Marsh, for "playing at crickets in a very unseemly fashion with boys and other very mean and base persons" on the Sabbath.

Evidence that the game was being taken seriously comes as early as 1646 when there was a court case over the non-payment of a cricket-related bet.

ABOVE 'Keeping The Wicket', a lady playing cricket c. 1850

THE LITTLE BOOK OF CRICKET 29

ORIGINS & DEVELOPMENT

Wagers became increasingly important, and by the end of the century there was a press report of an 11-a-side match in Sussex where the purse was "fifty guineas apiece". Cricket was becoming established in the social fabric.

Most of the early mentions of the game refer to Kent and Sussex, and it was in that region that it took shape as an organised sport. But as the 18th century progressed, London became more important. In the Regency era, the top echelons of the social strata liked nothing better than a substantial wager. Private clubs flourished and cricket, by now established as a bona fide, organised sport, represented another vehicle for gambling alongside horse racing. Sad to say, it also offered opportunities for corruption.

Wealthy patrons attracted the best players of the time to local clubs, so the village of Slindon near Arundel might take the field as Slindon, or the Duke of Richmond's side, or even Sussex. County identification was already strong, and Kent's game against Surrey at Dartford in 1709 is generally recognised as the first county match. The first mention of cricket at Cambridge University follows a year later.

There is written evidence from 1706 that there was an accepted form of the game and, if the Laws were not to be codified until 1744, the earlier document reveals that the various local versions of

ORIGINS & DEVELOPMENT

ABOVE A match between Sussex and Kent at Brighton by W H Mason (1849)

cricket had come together in a recognisable form. There were two batsmen, the ball was made of leather and bowled at a wicket comprising two stumps with a single bail across the top, and there were fielders, umpires and scorers.

In 1727, when the Duke of Richmond's team played against a side under the patronage of Mr. Broderick of Surrey, there were "Articles of

ORIGINS & DEVELOPMENT

Agreement" to govern the conduct of the match. The Laws might not have been in written form at this stage, but there was clearly an accepted way of playing.

Among the influential men of the time who took to cricket was the Prince of Wales, Frederick Louis. Not only did he lend his name to big matches, he played as well. Just six years before his father, George II, became the last British monarch to lead his troops into battle (at Dettingen against the French), Prince Frederick was leading Surrey against London at Moulsey Hurst, near Hampton Court.

Not only did the game stretch right across the social scale, from the Prince of Wales to tinkers, but it also attracted vast numbers of spectators. To discourage the riff-raff, admission charges were increased, but still the crowds came, hoping to recoup the considerable outlay to get into the ground by judicious wagers. Disappointment would often lead to spasmodic outbreaks of violence, or sometimes full-scale riots.

London was becoming the centre for cricket, but it was the provincial teams that held sway in terms of performance. By 1756, a team from Hambledon was emerging as the real power in the land.

In that year, a match against the leading Kent side, Dartford, was played at the Artillery Ground in London. It is an indication of the importance of the club from Hampshire that such a ground should be the venue for a match like this.

Hambledon played a significant part in cricket's development. Between 1772 and 1781, the village had a side featuring so many of the leading players of the day that they won 29 of the 51 matches played against All-England. The famous ground at Broadhalfpenny Down still exists, with the pub that formed its heart, the Bat and Ball, just over the road. It has changed little over some two centuries, and it is not difficult to imagine John Small, Richard Nyren, 'Silver' Billy Beldham and the rest in their pomp, beating the best of the rest in the land.

Gambling was almost the raison d'etre for cricket at the highest level, for as well as the even-sided matches there were single wicket contests or, say, five of one team with a couple of leading professionals from Hambledon, against another five with two more professionals who might also have come from Hambledon. Such matches were prime targets for rigging given the amounts being wagered on them; there is one account of a single-wicket encounter in which both a bowler and a batsman had been bribed to lose. It was, apparently, an unedifying spectacle!

Rather more legitimate instances of sharp practice led to modifications to the Laws. When batsmen began keeping balls from the wicket by using their legs (a somewhat painful exercise without pads!), it was deemed that deliberate use

ABOVE Frederick Louis, Prince of Wales, son of George II and father of George III, c. 1740

LEFT 'A gentleman playing cricket'. A drawing by John C Anderson, 1860

ABOVE W.G. Grace on the roof of the old pavilion at Lord's in 1895

of the leg to stop the ball hitting the stumps was out, leg before wicket. That was stipulated in the 1774 code that also limited the width of the bat to four and a quarter inches, a law that remains today. This was after a player by the name of 'Shock' White went to the middle with a bat that was wider than the wicket he was to defend.

There was another instance of a single incident leading to a change to the Laws. In 1775, Hambledon played Kent at the Artillery Ground. The last batsman for Hambledon made the 14 runs required to win despite the fact that he was 'bowled' three times during the course of his innings when the ball went between the two stumps without dislodging the bail. A third stump was introduced in 1776 to eliminate this anomaly.

Hambledon eventually vacated Broadhalfpenny Down in favour of neighbouring Windmill Down, but such was the interest in their matches that many were played in London. As the century reached its end, however, Hambledon's influence began to wane. London clubs were growing in importance, notably the Marylebone Club, which established itself at a new ground opened by Thomas Lord.

Lord was not notably successful as a player, but with the support of the Earl of Winchelsea and the Honourable Colonel Lennox, he opened a new ground where Dorset Square is now situated. Marylebone Cricket Club was formed in the year that the ground opened, 1787, and it was made their headquarters.

When Lord's ground, on which he had a lease, was sold for building, he took up the turf and replanted it half a mile northwards, establishing a new ground at North Bank. The MCC went with him, as they did when the new Regent's Canal was dug through the ground in 1814. Lord picked up his turf once again and, with the MCC in tow, took over a horticultural nursery in St. John's Wood. That is where Lord's Cricket Ground remains, where MCC still has its headquarters, and where the original use of the land is remembered by the Nursery End. By 1788, the MCC was influential enough to issue a revi-

ORIGINS & DEVELOPMENT

sion of the Laws, of which the club remains custodian today.

Throughout cricket's history, fundamental changes have been made, a process that continues to the present day. Many have come about to maintain the balance between bat and ball, so when the batsmen dominate, legislation comes in to encourage the bowlers, and vice versa. Thus it was that overarm bowling came into cricket.

At the outset, bowling had involved rolling the ball along the ground. Bowlers, however, searched for variations to baffle the batsmen. 'Length' bowling came into vogue, whereby the ball bounced. This allowed variations in flight, and turn became possible. Once the ball bounced, the old, curved bats became a thing of the past, as there was no longer a need to sweep the bat along the ground to make contact. It was more important to cover the bounce with a straight bat.

There is an apocryphal tale that roundarm bowling, the precursor of modern, overarm bowling, began when W.G. Grace's mother had bowled at her young son in the orchard of their home near Bristol. When her crinoline got in the way of bowling underarm, she resorted to lifting her arm to shoulder height to release the ball, and a new style was born.

Whatever else Mrs. Grace might have achieved in her life, she was not the originator of a new style of bowling. A number of professional bowlers in the early 1800s had toyed with the idea of overcoming the limitations of underarm bowling by raising their arm to shoulder level. The legislators responded by stipulating that the hand should be no higher than the elbow at the moment of release.

Such regulations did not always deter. John Willes of Kent bowled roundarm on and off in 1807 until he played against the MCC at Lord's in 1822. In a somewhat extreme reaction when his first delivery was called as a no ball, Willes threw away the ball, walked from the ground, mounted his horse and rode out of cricket. The scorecard supports the account in that it mentions Willes opening the bowling for Kent, but he did not appear in the batting order

BELOW William Lillywhite, who was largely responsible for the introduction of round-arm bowling, 1843

ABOVE A game at Lord's before fire destroyed the original pavilion later in 1825

bowling as legal in 1835. By 1864, overarm bowling was allowed and the game was well on its way to adopting a modern appearance.

As cricket became a major spectator sport crowds turned up to watch the big matches. There was North v South, Gentlemen against Players, Nottingham versus Sheffield and various MCC matches. Professionals who had made some money out of the game would often take a public house after their playing days, establish a cricket ground alongside and so became entrepreneurs.

The most successful of these was William Clarke. His path was a little different from normal as, in 1837, he married a widow who happened to own the Trent Bridge Inn in Nottingham, with an adjacent field that he turned into a cricket ground. A notable player himself, he lost an eye after an accident while playing fives as a youngster, but the remaining one was good for business.

Clarke introduced admission charges but the quality of the players he attracted was such that not long after he

or bowl in the MCC second innings.

Two Sussex professionals, William Lillywhite and James Broadbridge, tried to develop roundarm bowling and, after much debate, three experimental matches were staged to monitor the effect by pitting Sussex against England. Sussex won the first two, but were thwarted in the third when George Knight bowled roundarm for England.

The MCC was forced in 1828 to allow the bowler's hand to be as high as his elbow. Immediately the new Law was flouted, as most leading bowlers of the age went further and bowled from shoulder height with impunity. The MCC was forced to acknowledge such

ORIGINS & DEVELOPMENT

opened Trent Bridge that he was making spectators pay. Furthermore, he put together a touring side dubbed All-England that comprised some of the best players in the land. It was far too strong to take on local teams of 11, but against up to 22 players, including the odd professional, evenly matched contests could be contrived.

It was in 1846 that Clarke staged a benefit match (for himself, of course!) at Southwell, which enabled him to try out his idea of a touring circus. Considering it a success, he embarked on a tour of the north of England. The concept grew and he assembled a group of players who were unquestionably the best in England. Clarke insisted on a

BELOW The Bat and Ball Inn at Hambledon in 1908

ABOVE John Wisden, a successful bowler but best known as the founder of the Wisden Cricketers' Almanack, 1865

guarantee before the match, and usually made considerable amounts of money from each fixture.

Such was his control that when the MCC wanted to put out England sides to play the likes of Kent or Sussex, Clarke's men were enlisted to play. The fixture list was full, as were Clarke's coffers, although his players were stretched to the limit by the obligations placed upon them. Clarke did not spare himself either, taking the field regularly despite advancing years. In 1853, at the age of 54, he took 476 wickets. There was resentment that he did not always release his players for county matches, and in 1852 John Wisden, later of Almanack fame, was one of those who formed a rival group to Clarke called the United All-England XI.

Players in this group vowed never to play under Clarke's banner again, which made it impossible to for the two teams to meet. Clarke died in 1856, but not before taking a wicket with the last ball he ever bowled. In 1857, two matches were arranged at Lord's; Clarke's All-England XI won them both, but for several years, these matches were to be on a par with North v South and Gentlemen v Players as the grandest of fixtures.

Others tried to mine this profitable seam, but before long the public tired of the matches and instead warmed to the emerging contest that was county cricket and, later still, to Test cricket. In both cases, the Victorians' need for representative rather than commercial cricket was satisfied.

There was no definitive start to the County Championship. There had been county clubs since around 1825, when county cricket was first mentioned. With teams representing counties and the formation of county clubs, competitive cricket between them was bound to follow, but it was not until after the decline of the teams cobbled together for commercial purposes that county cricket assumed major importance. The last quarter of the 19th century, however, was the time for points rather than profit.

For many a year, talk of a Champion County was no more than an idle boast when a particular team had a good season. What approximated to the first

ORIGINS & DEVELOPMENT

county championship was determined in 1864. It was a rather haphazard affair, with Surrey declared champions after winning six and drawing their other two matches. Hampshire, Cambridgeshire, Sussex, Middlesex, Nottinghamshire, Kent and Yorkshire were the other sides involved.

Cambridgeshire had only a brief first-class existence, appearing in the championship from 1864 to 1869 and then again in 1871. In 1873, a meeting in London formulated some rules for the inauguration of a proper championship. Of the major counties, only Nottinghamshire failed to send a representative, while Gloucestershire sent a young man who had already made a name for himself, W.G. Grace. MCC was established as the arbitrator in any dispute over the running of the competition, if competition was not too grand a word for what was still a fairly loose association of clubs. Wisden, for example, did not contain a county table until 1888.

Nine counties were involved in the Championship from 1873. Derbyshire, Gloucestershire, Kent, Lancashire, Middlesex, Nottinghamshire, Surrey, Sussex and Yorkshire took part, with varied means of determining the champions. Fewest defeats featured as one, while sometimes most wins formed the criterion. At one point Derbyshire, after winning only one match in four seasons, were replaced by Somerset, but they were back in 1895 along with Essex, Hampshire, Leicestershire and Warwickshire.

BELOW An England team assembled at Lord's before leaving for the 1863 tour of Australia. Back row (left to right) Julius Caesar, Alfred Clarke, George Tarrant, George Parr, E M Grace, Robert Carpenter, George Anderson, William Caffyn; (front row) Robert C Tinley, Thomas Lockyer, Thomas Hayward, John Jackson

THE LITTLE BOOK OF CRICKET 39

ORIGINS & DEVELOPMENT

1895 marks, for many, the start of the Championship proper. Points became the measure of success, with one awarded for a win, one deducted for a defeat, and drawn games not counting. The final table was determined by the greatest number of points gained in proportion to the number of finished matches. The number taking part rose to 15 in 1899 when Worcestershire were admitted, followed by Northamptonshire in 1905. Glamorgan's inclusion in 1921 boosted the total to 17, and there it stayed until 1992 when Durham were awarded first-class status.

The balance of power has shifted over the years, with Yorkshire the champions in eight seasons out of ten between 1931 and 1946, while Surrey enjoyed unprecedented dominance in the 1950s, taking seven successive titles. Since the modern Championship began in 1895, all the counties except Durham, Gloucestershire, Northamptonshire and Somerset have taken at least one title. The challenge to do so became sterner in 2000 when the Championship was split into two divisions.

For sides that find the longer form of the game too demanding, there have been other opportunities to win silverware since the inauguration of the Gillette Cup in 1963. At a time when the county game was in serious decline, one-day cricket proved to be a lifesaver. It was fairly low-key at first, with 65-over matches in the first year, reduced to 60 overs the following season. It remained as such until matches were reduced to 50 overs a side in 1999.

By then, the competition had changed sponsorship, becoming the NatWest Trophy in 1981 and the Cheltenham and Gloucester Trophy in 2001 but whichever banner was flown, the competition still evoked excitement. Sussex were the early leading practitioners and Lancashire inherited the mantle, winning seven of their ten finals, while Gloucestershire and Warwickshire each had five successes to their name by the time the competition was radically altered for the 2006 season. It was no longer to be a straight knockout tournament; the first stage became a two-division league, with the winners of each table meeting in the final.

ABOVE The badge worn on the caps of the England team, 1953

RIGHT The Twenty20 trophy is unveiled in 2003

40 THE LITTLE BOOK OF CRICKET

No domestic limited-overs competition has endured more structural changes than what was generically known as the Sunday League. The new limited-overs league began life in 1969 as "The Player's County League". It was changed to the John Player League in 1970 to end any impression that it was the players themselves who were behind it.

It grew out of another tobacco-sponsored series of matches, involving the Rothman's Cavaliers. Before regular Sunday afternoon cricket, the Cavaliers, made up of some of the biggest names of the day, overseas players and some past greats, travelled the country playing for beneficiaries and other charitable causes in front of the television cameras. It was such a success that an organised competition was bound to follow. The public loved it and county cricket was given a new lease of life. "Ground Full" notices had to be improvised, and for a top-of-the-table clash towards the end of the season it was not unknown for spectators to arrive in the early hours to ensure a good seat.

The competition went through several incarnations. It became the John Player Special League, the Refuge Assurance League, with an associated

ORIGINS & DEVELOPMENT

cup for the top four at the end of the season, the AXA Equity and Law League, the AXA Life League, the AXA League, CGU National League, the Norwich Union National League, Norwich Union League and the totesport League. There were two seasons when a sponsor could not be found, so it was known as the Sunday League (its most familiar title anyway) and the National League.

The basis for its success was its simplicity. 40 overs a side, bowlers limited to a 15-yard run-up, and two o'clock starts every Sunday. Then some who should have known better began to cast aspersions. Changes were made, with bowlers allowed to come off an unlimited run, matches started earlier, and it became a 50-over competition in 1993 before falling back to 45.

As the media gave it less exposure, the public started to lose interest, and the advent of coloured clothing failed to arrest the decline. Matches were played on different days of the week, some under floodlights, which had a certain novelty appeal. The introduction of two divisions was meant to revive interest, but too much tinkering resulted in too little progress. By the time the 2006 season came around, the Sunday League had become somewhat marginalized in the second half of the season and known as the NatWest Pro 40.

1972 saw the start of the third limited-overs competition in English

ORIGINS & DEVELOPMENT

ABOVE
Nottinghamshire celebrate winning the County Championship in 2005

cricket, the Benson and Hedges Cup. It began on a league basis, with the country divided into qualifying groups before a knockout format in the later stages, with 55 overs available between 1972 and 1995. It then fell in line with international limited-overs cricket with 50 overs.

The B&H never quite had the kudos of the senior knockout trophy, but it earned its keep before the authorities decided that tobacco sponsorship

ORIGINS & DEVELOPMENT

ABOVE Wasim Akram of Lancashire holds the trophy after winning the 1998 AXA League

RIGHT The Lord's Taverners trophy for the winners of the County Championship

should be phased out of English sport. It coughed and spluttered in 1999 when it was branded, none too convincingly, the Benson and Hedges Super Cup – irreverently dubbed "the Superfluous Cup". Only the top eight teams from the previous season's Championship quali-fied. It returned to normal for the next three seasons before it was finally stubbed out in 2002.

It was replaced in 2003 by a new competition designed to appeal to the non-cricketing public. The Twenty20 arrived on a wave of publicity and gimmicks. Whatever the purists thought, it was commercially very successful and undoubtedly exciting as a spectacle. It was like the early days of the Sunday League, and there were numerous occasions when those old "Ground Full" notices were dusted down and displayed once again.

As cricket spread around the world, the leading countries copied England. Just as the County Championship evolved, so did state or provincial cricket in what were then the colonies. Australia had the Sheffield Shield, South Africa the Currie Cup, the Plunkett Shield developed in New Zealand and so on. Just as in England, sponsorship changed the names as one-day competitions joined the first-class championships. What is the latest version to

ORIGINS & DEVELOPMENT

spread around the world? Twenty20, which quickly attained international status as well as domestic acclaim.

Administration has been copied as well, although most overseas countries managed to avoid many of the pitfalls encountered in England as the game developed. It was very much a free-for-all in the early days before the MCC emerged as the governing body. It remained so in England until the formation of the Test and County Cricket Board in 1968, and also administered the International Cricket Council until 1993. The MCC also ran tours undertaken by England until 1979, when it ceded control to the TCCB.

The TCCB was formed as the first-class arm of the Cricket Council, with the National Cricket Association responsible for the game below first-class level. That situation endured until 1997, when the England and Wales Cricket Board came into existence. The establishment of the ECB, which has itself undergone change since, brought the game in England closer to being administered by a single body. Would those shepherds playing on the downs have ever believed that their simple pastime would assume such huge proportions?

Chapter 3

Test Cricket

RIGHT Yorkshire's Arthur Lupton with England Test cricketers George Hirst and Wilfred Rhodes at Lord's, 1920

SINCE THE FIRST-EVER TEST match in 1877, in which Australia beat England by 45 runs at Melbourne, over 1,800 contests have been played between ten different nations. Despite the popularity of one-day internationals in recent years, Test cricket is still the most highly regarded form of the game

England's defeat at Melbourne – avenged the following month – preceded another two years later, in which the legendary Australian fast bowler Frederick Spofforth took the first-ever Test hat-trick among his 13 wickets in the match. The England team to host Australia in 1880 included W.G. Grace, who made 152 on Test debut, although Australia's captain, Billy Murdoch, bettered this by one run, enabling his team to give England a fright before capitulating. Spofforth featured in the classic Oval encounter in 1882 which England lost by just seven runs.

The tiny Ashes urn came into being the following winter. Ivo Bligh led a team to Australia that avenged the earlier reversal by winning a three-match rubber 2-1, and was presented with the urn by a group of women who had been following the series. It contained the ashes of a bail, or perhaps a ball, or possibly the veil of one of the ladies, Florence Rose Murphy, who was to become Bligh's wife. She bequeathed it to the MCC, and it is now kept in the Lord's museum.

Bligh's revenge owed much to the batting of Walter Read and the all-round contributions of Allan Steel. The rubber was England's 2-1, and the Ashes had been won for the first time. England were to hold them for almost a decade. Steel made 148 in their Lord's win in 1884 that secured the next series, while George Ulyett's seven for 36 included a brilliant catch off a fierce

THE LITTLE BOOK OF CRICKET 47

TEST CRICKET

ABOVE Australia's Frederick Spofforth, 1880

return drive from George Bonnor.

England were led by Arthur Shrewsbury, one of the finest batsmen of his generation, in their 3-2 win in 1884/85, in which the bowling of Bobby Peel was a significant factor. In 1886 an injury to Spofforth hampered the Australian tourists, while Shrewsbury and Grace contributed to wins at Lord's and the Oval. Not even the all-round heroics of George Giffen could save Australia; nor, in 1886/87, did the emergence of the bowling duo of Charlie Turner and J.J. Ferris prevent a 2-0 defeat.

It was Turner and Ferris who brought a temporary end to Australia's misery at Lord's in 1888, with 18 wickets between them on a damp pitch. But England, now led by Grace, struck back at the Oval through the bowling of Peel, Billy Barnes and Johnny Briggs, before Peel snared 11 batsmen in an innings victory at Old Trafford.

England first met South Africa at Port Elizabeth and Cape Town in March 1889. The team was not the strongest available, but they comfortably won both matches. The 1890 Ashes series was closer; Grace saw England to a seven-wicket win at Lord's but the Oval Test was another nail-biter. Set 95 to win England only narrowly avoided a repeat of the 1882 outcome, as Turner and Ferris brought Australia within just two wickets of triumph.

Improved batting in 1891/92, led by Alec Bannerman and John Lyons, set up Australian wins at Melbourne and Sydney, and although the bat of Andrew Stoddart and the bowling of Briggs gave Grace's England victory in the last game, the Ashes were back with Australia. England regained them little more than a year later thanks to a solitary win at the Oval, which included ten more scalps for Briggs and a century from Stanley Jackson.

Stoddart's England played an engaging five-Test rubber in 1894/95, winning the first match at Sydney after being forced to follow on. Giffen and Syd Gregory set up a total of 580 for Australia, but England battled to such effect in both innings that the hosts were left needing 177 to win. They fell ten runs short. England went two up at Melbourne but fell foul of the debutant Albert Trott in Adelaide. Rain helped Australia win at the SCG, but England won a fine decider back in Melbourne to clinch the rubber 3-2.

They retained the Ashes back home in 1896, after 11 wickets for Tom Richardson set up a win at Lord's. Australia hit back at Old Trafford despite a stellar England debut from the Indian prince K.S. Ranjitsinhji (Ranji),

ABOVE 'Plum' Warner of Middlesex and England, 1910

THE LITTLE BOOK OF CRICKET **49**

TEST CRICKET

RIGHT Australia's Billy Murdoch (wearing cap) and England's W.G. Grace (with beard) at Crystal Palace cricket ground, 1900

who made 62 and 154 not out. But ten wickets for Jack Hearne and eight for Peel sealed it at the Oval by 66 runs.

England's opening win in Sydney in 1897/98 turned out to be a flash in the pan, as Australia won the next four matches off the reel. They won again on their next visit in 1899, in the first five-Test rubber played in England. It featured Grace's final Test at Trent Bridge, where Wilfred Rhodes and Victor Trumper made their debuts. Trumper and Clem Hill both hit 135 in the decisive win at Lord's.

Australia confirmed their growing strength against Archie MacLaren's England in 1901/02. England were hard hit by an injury to Sydney Barnes, who took 19 wickets before succumbing to knee trouble. Five came in England's opening win at the SCG but Australia won the remaining four Tests. They were again too strong in 1902, prevailing in Sheffield and at Old Trafford when Fred Tate, England's number eleven, famously fell to a shooter from Jack Saunders. Another thriller followed at the Oval, with England getting home thanks to a century from Gilbert Jessop, and George Hirst, who with 15 runs

TEST CRICKET

needed, reportedly said to the incoming number eleven, Wilfred Rhodes: "We'll get 'em in singles!"

Pelham Warner's England won 3-2 in 1903/04, thanks in part to the efforts of the inventor of the googly, B.J.T. Bosanquet. In 1905 they prevailed again, owing largely to Jackson, who topped both batting and bowling averages. South Africa's first Test success came against Warner's England team in 1905/06 – they won the series 4-1 - but their batsmen, with the shining exception of the great Herbie Taylor, were soon to fall under the spell of Barnes, who struck 34 times in the triangular series of 1912 and reaped an astounding 49 wickets in four Tests in 1913/14.

Australia triumphed by four to one in 1907/08. Jack Hobbs made 83 on debut in England's one victory, in the second match at the MCG. Australia won again in 1909 despite going behind to the bowling of Hirst and Colin Blythe in the first Test at Edgbaston. Victories at Lord's and Headingley took them in front, before draws at Old Trafford and the Oval.

One of the great bowling partnerships, that of Barnes and Frank Foster,

ABOVE Fans queuing for the Test between England and South Africa at Lord's, 1935

turned the 1911/12 series on its head after Johnny Douglas's England went behind in Sydney. While the former provided swing and spin from the right arm, the latter generated pace from the left. The batting of Hobbs and Rhodes also assisted England to a 4-1 win. After such a compelling series the 1912 triangular tournament was anti-climactic. A weakened Australia had the worst of the one result, at the Oval where the Kent left-hander Frank Woolley scored 62 and took ten wickets.

The intervention of the war prevented any further contests until 1920/21, by which time Australia were

TEST CRICKET

to overwhelm England, despite the efforts of Hobbs and the captain, Johnny Douglas. The following summer England, without Hobbs, went down 3-0.

Fortunes failed to improve when Arthur Gilligan's team visited Australia in 1924/25. The fast bowling of Maurice Tate, who took 38 wickets, the reliability of Hobbs and the emergence of Herbert Sutcliffe provided the few encouraging elements as Australia won 4-1. Sutcliffe scored 143 towards England's 548 which set up their one win, by an innings, at the MCG. The wheel at last turned in 1926 as Australia were held for four Tests and then beaten at the Oval. The recall of Rhodes at the age of 49 proved inspirational after one of Hobbs and Sutcliffe's finest stands – 172 on a damp wicket – left Australia needing 415. Rhodes bowled his team to victory in his final bow.

led by the "Big Ship" Warwick Armstrong. He scored 158 as England were well beaten in the first Test, and the outcome was no different over the next four. The fast bowling of Jack Gregory, who from mid-series was partnered by Ted McDonald, combined with the spin of Arthur Mailey

THE LITTLE BOOK OF CRICKET **53**

TEST CRICKET

The West Indies first played Test cricket in 1928, their team including the all-rounder Learie Constantine, the prototype of crowd pleasers. He made an explosive impact against Middlesex at Lord's, scoring 86 in an hour, taking seven for 57 and then a decisive 103, again in an hour. Although he was less influential in the Tests – his team was beaten by an innings in all three – he epitomised the brilliance in the field that was already a feature of Caribbean cricket.

Percy Chapman led England to a 4-1 win Down Under in 1928/29. The pace of Harold Larwood was critical, supported by Tate and the left arm spin of Jack White. Walter Hammond emerged as a batting colossus, with 251 in Sydney, 200 in Melbourne, followed by 119 and 177 at Adelaide. No less relevant to the future, though, was the appearance of Don Bradman, whose century in the final match at the MCG led to Australia's one victory.

England's Caribbean visit in 1929/30 resulted in an evenly matched rubber of five Tests. The last, with the teams all square at one-all, was timeless, and notable for Freddie Calthorpe's decision not to enforce

TEST CRICKET

the follow-on after the hosts had replied to England's 849 with just 286. George Headley made 223 in their second innings, and after rain on day eight England's players had to catch the boat home. They were not at full strength, as the MCC also sent a team to New Zealand that winter to play in four Tests. The hosts were dispatched in bleak weather at Christchurch, the only result of the rubber.

When Bill Woodfull's Australians toured England in 1930 Bradman's hundred at Trent Bridge was unavailing, but his insatiable appetite for runs was revealed at Lord's. The 173 made for England by another Indian prince - K.S. Duleepsinhji – paled by comparison as Bradman made 254 out of a match-winning 729, and he went 80 better at Headingley, breaking the world Test record. His 232 at the Oval set up a triumph for the old enemy.

New Zealand's pre-war batting legend was Stewie Dempster, who averaged a shade under 60 in 1931, including a century at Lord's, as the tourists played well enough for two more Tests to be added to the schedule. They were outplayed at the Oval and saved by the weather against Douglas Jardine's England the following winter. Hammond dipped the bread in both Tests, with 227 and 336 not out, then the highest individual score. India's first Test was at Lord's in 1932, a one-off encounter won by England.

It was clear, meanwhile, that in Don

ABOVE Fast bowler Harold Larwood had a recorded bowling speed of over 90 miles per hour

LEFT Australian opening batsmen Bill Woodfull (left) and Archie Jackson going out to bat against Worcestershire in 1930

TEST CRICKET

ABOVE Lala Amarnath during the All-India tour of England, 1936

Bradman England's bowlers were up against a virtually irresistible force. Jardine's team responded in 1932/33 with a strategy that embroiled cricket in what probably remains its greatest collective controversy. Now known as 'Bodyline', it involved fast, short deliveries, mainly from Larwood and Bill Voce, aimed at the batsman's body, with a ring of close fielders on the leg side. It worked in so far as England won the series 4-1, but the cost to relations between the two countries was huge.

Bradman missed the Sydney Test, in which the brave hooking of Stan McCabe, who made 187, merely delayed Australia's defeat. Larwood and Voce took 16 of the 20 wickets. At the MCG 'The Don' made up for a duck with a second innings ton, and ten wickets for the leg spinner Bill O'Reilly restored parity. But it was on a lively pitch at Adelaide that the pot boiled over. With Larwood bowling to an orthodox field, Woodfull was hit on the chest. Jardine reverted to a bodyline field, and to the crowd's fury the Australian captain was peppered with short deliveries.

There was further uproar the following day when Bert Oldfield was injured as he top-edged a Larwood bouncer into his face. The match, which England won, prompted an exchange of telegrams between the Australian Cricket Board and MCC. England also prevailed at Brisbane and Sydney, but never have the Ashes been won at such a cost. Bradman still averaged over 56

ABOVE New Zealand's Jack Cowie in the nets

in the series, after which MCC resolved "that any form of bowling which is obviously a direct attack … upon the batsman would be an offence against the spirit of the game." Larwood, who took 33 wickets, did not play Test cricket again.

England overpowered the West Indies in 1933, and won 2-0 in India in 1933/34, although an aggressive century on debut by Lala Amarnath held them up in Bombay. The slow left arm bowler Hedley Verity took 11 wickets as England won the third Test in Madras. Meanwhile Australia were not slow to take revenge. O'Reilly and Clarrie Grimmett span England to perdition at Trent Bridge in 1934, although Verity took advantage of a wet wicket at Lord's, taking 15 wickets to ensure that centuries from Maurice Leyland and Les Ames did not go to waste. At Headingley Bradman scored 304, adding 388 for the fourth wicket with Bill Ponsford (181). The pair did even better at the Oval, with a second wicket partnership of 451.

THE LITTLE BOOK OF CRICKET **57**

Ponsford made 266 and Bradman 244 before O'Reilly and Grimmett ensured the Ashes' return to the Antipodes. England would not regain them for 19 years.

Headley's Herculean batting at last reaped dividends in the Caribbean in 1934/35. His unbeaten 270 in Jamaica ensured a 2-1 win after England had led through victory on a wet pitch in Barbados, and Constantine's 121 runs and five wickets in Trinidad had helped his team straight back. And after 28 years of trying, South Africa won their first Test in England at Lord's in 1935. Xenophon Balaskas, a leg spinner of Greek origin who took nine wickets, was pivotal in securing their first series win in England. The following summer England won 2-0 against an Indian team riven by internal strife.

In Australia in 1936/37 their captain Gubby Allen helped to restore relations. He and Voce bowled England into the lead after a Maurice Leyland century at Brisbane, and helped by rain and Hammond (231) extended that at the SCG. Rain aided Australia in Melbourne, bedevilling a pitch on which England were bowled out for 76. A record partnership of 346 between Bradman and Jack Fingleton put the match beyond England, who fell foul of another Bradman double century, and the spin of O'Reilly and 'Chuck' Fleetwood-Smith, at the Adelaide Oval. Australia clinched an engrossing rubber back at the MCG, where Bradman (169) set up the same two bowlers.

In 1937 the efforts of New Zealand's fast bowler Jack Cowie at Old Trafford came to nothing as they were spun to defeat by Tom Goddard. The last Ashes contest before the Second World War is memorable for Len Hutton's 364, which helped England to 903 for seven at the Oval. Hutton's innings of over 13 hours, combined with injuries to Bradman and Fingleton, squared the series.

England's tour of South Africa in 1938/39 featured the "timeless Test" in Durban, one of the freaks of cricket

ABOVE Joe Hardstaff Junior of Nottinghamshire and England

RIGHT West Indian batsman Clyde Walcott

58 THE LITTLE BOOK OF CRICKET

TEST CRICKET

history. England were set 696 to win it, and were within striking distance at 654 for five (on day ten!) when rain intervened. Unfortunately the game could not continue, as England had to catch the boat home. Hutton and Denis Compton contributed to England's 1-0 win over the West Indies in 1939; after Constantine's whirlwind 79 in his last Test, the tour was truncated by the threat of war.

The senior Nawab of Pataudi led India in 1946. The series was a particular triumph for Alec Bedser, who combined with Joe Hardstaff junior (205), to win the first Test for England at Lord's, the one result of the rubber. The haste to resume Ashes rivalry after the war probably contributed to England's failure in Australia in 1946/47. The arrival of Ray Lindwall and Keith Miller boosted Australia, while Bradman was still not done with England's attack. Although there were runs from Compton and wickets for Doug Wright and Bedser, England were beaten 3-0.

England's trip to the Caribbean in 1947/48 ushered in the era of the "Three Ws". Frank Worrell came within three runs of a century on

TEST CRICKET

debut in Georgetown, and made sure of the landmark in the next game, helping his team to a 1-0 lead. The batting of Everton Weekes (141) ensured a 2-0 win against an England team lacking several frontline players ahead of the resumption of Ashes rivalry the following summer. Clyde Walcott was to post his first three-figure score on the tour of India that followed.

Australian were known as 'The Invincibles' by Bradman's final tour in 1948. England were beaten at Headingley despite 184 from Compton, and trounced at Lord's. At Headingley, Bradman played his last great innings of 173, joining Arthur Morris (182) to complete one of Test cricket's great run chases. The Oval Test is remembered for an incomparable piece of drama, but not before Lindwall's inspirational six for 20 reduced England to 52 all out. By the time Bradman batted Australia's total was already double that, and it was clear that this would be his last Test innings. Needing just four to lift his average above 100, he was cheered all the way to the wicket, only to be bowled, second ball, by Eric Hollies for a duck. Morris's 196 set up an innings win, and Australia had taken four Tests in England for the first time.

The famous phrase "Cometh the hour, cometh the man" was coined by Cliff Gladwin on England's 1948/49 tour of South Africa, in one of the tensest finishes ever. England were set 128 to win in 135 minutes, and Gladwin, batting at number nine, found himself facing the last ball with just one run needed. He and Alec Bedser scampered the single after the ball hit his thigh, and performed a celebratory one-step as they left the field. Bert Sutcliffe scored over 2,600 runs on New Zealand's tour of England in 1949, which ended in stalemate.

The watershed in Anglo-Caribbean rivalry came in 1950, along with the "little pals of mine",

TEST CRICKET

Ramadhin and Valentine. At Old Trafford Alf Valentine took eight wickets in 50 overs of slow left-arm while Sonny Ramadhin snared the other two with his concoction of off spin and leg breaks. At Lord's they took 18 wickets between them, propelling the West Indies to a comprehensive win. With the help of a partnership of 283 between Worrell and Weekes they prevailed again at Trent Bridge, and demolished England at the Oval.

In 1950/51 Australia started with a win on a Brisbane 'sticky dog', despite a defiant 62 from Hutton. Penetrative bowling from Bedser and Trevor Bailey could not prevent another defeat in Melbourne, and a white-hot match for Miller - four for 37 and 145 not out - made it 3-0 at the SCG. A Morris double century set up another win at Adelaide, although a ten-wicket haul for Bedser gave England a consolation win in the final Test.

South Africa's second win in England came at Trent Bridge in 1951, thanks largely to Dudley Nourse's 208. Nonetheless, the rubber was won comfortably by the hosts. In India in 1951/52, Vinoo Mankad took 34 wickets

LEFT West Indian left-arm spinner Alf Valentine

TEST CRICKET

ABOVE South Africa captain Dudley Nourse at the crease, 1951

in five Tests. The visitors won the fourth in Kanpur, but centuries from Pankaj Roy and Polly Umrigar set up an innings victory for India in Madras, where Mankad took 12 wickets to seal the first Test win in India's history. The following summer Fred Trueman, on Test debut, reduced India to 0 for 4 in their second innings at Headingley. England won there, and at Lord's despite the heroics of Mankad, who made 72 and 184, and took five wickets as England amassed an unassailable 537. At Old Trafford Trueman and Bedser were too much for India's batsmen.

In 1953, England hung in with Australia before striking at the finish. Bedser took 14 wickets at Trent Bridge and eight more at Lord's, where the immortal stand of 163 in more than four hours between Bailey and Willie Watson saved England's bacon. Bedser's efforts were complemented by Trueman at the Oval where, after a captain's 82 from Hutton, the spin of Jim Laker and Tony Lock wrapped up Australia for 162, leaving England only 132 to win. Australia refused to give it away, making England fight for three and a half hours. When Compton hit the winning runs it must have felt like a national catharsis; 15,000 people thronged the pavilion to salute England's first Ashes-winning heroes for more than two decades.

Despite another command performance by the 'Three Ws' in the Caribbean in 1953/54, Hutton led an England fightback with 169 in British Guiana and 205 in Jamaica, both of which set up wins. The other key performance at Kingston came from Bailey, who took seven for 34 on day one as the hosts crumbled for 139.

The medium pace bowler Fazal Mahmood struck 20 times in Pakistan's first Test series in England in 1954. Compton made his best Test score of 278 at Trent Bridge as Pakistan subsided by an innings, and at the Oval they looked to be going the same way when they were dismissed for 133. But after a cloudburst prevented any play on day two, Fazal and Mahmood Hussain restricted England to just 130. Only Compton, with a masterful half century, withstood them. On a drying pitch, the spin of Johnny Wardle took seven wickets as Pakistan, 82 for eight at one stage, eventually reached 164, leaving England 168 to win. Six more wickets for Fazal left them 24 short and Pakistan were the first team to win a Test in their first rubber in England.

Despite an initial setback in Brisbane England extended their Ashes dominance in 1954/55. The express pace of Frank Tyson, together

ABOVE Mahmood Hussain of Pakistan

ABOVE South African wicket-keeper Russell Endean, 1955

with an innings of 104 from Peter May, restored parity in a Sydney thriller. After a century from the 20-year-old Colin Cowdrey Tyson blew Australia away in Melbourne, and the Ashes were clinched at Adelaide. England then won in New Zealand, who were dismissed for 26 in their second innings at Auckland, Test cricket's lowest-ever total.

England triumphed over South Africa again in 1955, although the margin of 3-2 reflected their opponents' steady improvement, particularly in the field. Laker's match at Old Trafford, when the off-spinner took 19 wickets, ensured the retention of the Ashes in 1956. The bowling of Miller had put Australia one up at Lord's, but England had levelled things at Headingley before Laker weaved his magical web.

The fading of the 'Three Ws', along with Ramadhin and Valentine, contributed to the West Indies' 3-0 defeat in 1957. England's psychological breakthrough was the stand of 411 between May and Cowdrey in the first Test at Edgbaston, taming Ramadhin after he had taken seven for 49 in the first innings. It remains an England record, and almost stole the match before England won three of the remaining four by an innings.

Thanks mainly to Laker and Lock (51 Test wickets between them) and May, who scored 777 runs against them in eight first-class innings, England won all but one of the five Tests against New Zealand in 1958, and six months

TEST CRICKET

later Lock took 11 wickets to ensure victory at Christchurch after Ted Dexter's maiden Test century.

Australia's renaissance in 1958/59 owed much to the captaincy of Richie Benaud, who took seven wickets with his leg spin to wrest the initiative in Brisbane. At Melbourne it was the faster bowlers, Alan Davidson and Ian Meckiff, who unstitched England, and Colin McDonald made 170 at Adelaide before Benaud came to the fore again back at the MCG, claiming nine victims as the tourists surrendered the small urn once more. In 1959, May's England overpowered India from the moment when Trueman, now in harness with Brian Statham, reasserted himself in the first Test.

England triumphed in the Caribbean in 1959/60 despite Garry Sobers' 709 runs at an average a shade over 100. The key game in Trinidad was held up on the third afternoon by bottle throwing, after the hosts had collapsed to Trueman and Statham. England eventually won by 256 runs. The following season the West Indies featured in one of the greatest Tests, the tie in Brisbane that yielded 1,474 runs before the 40th wicket fell with the scores level on the final day.

Australia won 2-1 in 1961, Davidson and Graham McKenzie bowling them to a 1-0 win at Lord's, and after England had hit back at Leeds, primarily through

BELOW Graham McKenzie makes a 'blind' catch to dismiss England's Tom Graveney, 1968

ABOVE South African fast bowler Peter Pollock

RIGHT Colin Bland, nicknamed the 'Golden Eagle', 1965

Trueman's 11 wickets, Benaud's decision to bowl round the wicket into the bowlers' footmarks at Old Trafford conjured a crucial win for Australia which was to settle the series. His six victims included Ted Dexter, whose daring 76 had threatened to win a fine match for England in double quick time.

Bizarrely, the first Test of England's 1961/62 visit to Pakistan, in Lahore, preceded five Tests in India, before England returned to complete the three-match series. They won by five wickets; centuries from Javed Burki and Ken Barrington left things evenly matched on first innings before the spin of David Allen and Bob Barber dismissed Pakistan for 200 in the second. An unbeaten 66 from Dexter saw England home and sealed the rubber. Meanwhile in India after three drawn Tests they were well beaten in the fourth at Calcutta, where a dashing century by the junior Nawab of Pataudi set up India's first series win over England.

The win over Pakistan the next summer was comprehensive. Centuries from Cowdrey and Peter Parfitt led to an innings win at Edgbaston, and Burki's decision to bat on a lively Lord's wicket backfired, with Trueman taking six for 31 as they were bowled out for 100. 153 from Tom Graveney enhanced English hopes of another innings win, but Burki and Nasim-ul-

TEST CRICKET

Ghani each made 101 in Pakistan's second innings, which at least forced England to bat again. A dismal display by the tourists resulted in a three-day win for England at Headingley; Parfitt again reached three figures, and big hundreds from Cowdrey and Dexter provided the foundations for a ten-wicket win at the Oval.

Dexter's batting, along with that of Cowdrey and David Sheppard, helped put England one up in the second 1962/63 Ashes Test at the MCG, but Australia's riposte was swift. High-class bowling from Davidson and McKenzie skittled them in Sydney, giving Australia an eight-wicket victory, the last result of the series. A rain-plagued rubber followed in England in 1964 that produced just one result, a win for Australia at Headingley. Fred Trueman became England's leading wicket-taker in New Zealand, where two of the three matches were won by an innings.

Worrell's farewell to England in 1963 was a triumphant one for the West Indies. The 83-ball innings of 70 played in the thrilling draw at Lord's by Dexter, now England's captain, was a highlight of a series that they lost

TEST CRICKET

ABOVE Barry Richards in action for Hampshire, 1964

game's place in cricketing immortality. A winter stalemate followed in India, where all five Tests were drawn.

England's victory in the first Test of the 1964/65 tour of South Africa was decisive, but South Africa won the return 1965 rubber by the same margin. A new generation was emerging that included the Pollock brothers, batsman Graham and pace bowler Peter, all-rounder Eddie Barlow and peerless fielder Colin Bland, who brilliantly ran out Barrington in the drawn first Test at Lord's. It was the Pollocks who set up South Africa's win at Trent Bridge. Another 3-0 thrashing of New Zealand preceded the South Africa series; founded on the batting of Barrington and John Edrich, who made 310 at Headingley.

As on their previous trip to Australia three years earlier, England failed to convert a 1-0 lead in 1965/66. Australia were outplayed at Sydney, but again found the resolve to bounce back at Adelaide. Bobby Simpson and Bill Lawry put on 244 for the first wicket, more than England's total, and despite resistance from Barrington (109), Australia won without batting again, McKenzie and Neil Hawke shar-

3-1. That, Brian Close's second innings 70 and Cowdrey's emergence with a broken arm to stand at the non-striker's end while David Allen played out the last over, ensured the

TEST CRICKET

ing 13 wickets. A stalemate in New Zealand followed.

When the West Indies toured England in 1966 Sobers was in his prime, making 722 runs and taking 20 wickets in various styles. His team was far too strong for a disoriented England, led by three captains and with 23 different players. But England resumed business as usual against India in 1967. Geoff Boycott was dropped for slow scoring after making 246 not out in nine and a half hours at Headingley in the first Test, which England won by six wickets. At Lord's they did it more easily, Ray Illingworth spinning them to an innings win after Tom Graveney had made 151. England completed a clean sweep at Edgbaston. Pakistan fared little better than India; their best effort coming in the drawn first Test at Lord's, where Hanif Mohammad scored 187. But at Trent Bridge they were undone, first by the seam of Geoff Arnold and Ken Higgs, then by the spin of Derek Underwood. Arnold and Higgs again exposed the tourists' batting frailty at the Oval.

The 1967/68 series in the Caribbean was memorable for a sporting declaration by Sobers in the fourth Test at Trinidad, which left England needing

ABOVE Basil D'Oliveira in action for England at the Oval in 1965. Barry Jarman is keeping wicket

TEST CRICKET

215 in 165 minutes to win a game that had looked to be heading for a draw. Sobers was short of firepower and well-paced innings by Cowdrey and Boycott saw England home, to the outrage of the Caribbean cricket-loving public. Despite brilliant batting by Kanhai and Sobers in the final Test at Georgetown, England saved the game through Cowdrey and Alan Knott to ensure a 1-0 series win.

Australia went one up at Old Trafford in 1968, as Bob Cowper and McKenzie took 11 wickets between them. The series ended with one of the most dramatic of all Ashes encounters at the Oval. England led through Edrich (164) and Basil D'Oliveira (158), but were then dismissed for 181, leaving Australia needing 352 for victory. A storm on the fifth morning appeared to have ended the match, but scores of volunteers helped mop up the water. In conditions made for him Underwood ripped through Australia to give England victory and a share in the rubber.

The next winter England were scheduled to tour South Africa, whose government's policy of apartheid was by now causing international offence.

It was put under the spotlight by the emergence in England of D'Oliveira, who was born in Cape Town but denied the chance to play cricket there on account of his colour. Following his inclusion in the tour squad, the South African government made it clear that a team with D'Oliveira in it would not be welcome. The MCC responded by cancelling the tour.

By 1970, when South Africa were next due to tour England, a series of anti-apartheid demonstrations had already disrupted the 1969/70 Springbok rugby tour of Britain, and a "Stop the Seventy Tour" committee was established. 13 African countries threatened to boycott the Commonwealth Games if the tour went ahead and eventually the invitation to tour was withdrawn. South Africa were not to play Test cricket for 22 years, and as a result the international standing of some great cricketers, including Barry Richards and Mike Procter, is immeasurable.

Instability in Pakistan when England visited in 1968/69 disrupted all the Tests. Rioting held up an intriguing first match in Lahore, and time ran out at Dacca on a bowler-dominated second Test in which D'Oliveira scored a century. Colin Milburn and Graveney both reached three figures in Karachi, but a riot forced the early abandonment of the match and the tour. A hiatus in the West Indies' attack resulted in a 2-0 loss in England in 1969, before Underwood fully deserved his nickname of "Deadly" against New Zealand. On two

ABOVE England batsman Colin Milburn back in training after a car accident in which he lost his left eye

LEFT A demonstrator is carried off at an anti-apartheid protest at Swansea, 1969

THE LITTLE BOOK OF CRICKET 71

TEST CRICKET

ABOVE Ken Barrington presents Zaheer Abbas with an award

RIGHT Bev Congdon of New Zealand

helpful pitches, at Lord's and the Oval, he took 23 wickets.

England's recovery of the Ashes in 1970/71 owed much to the captaincy of Ray Illingworth, the batting of Boycott and the fast bowling of John Snow. Boycott anchored England at the SCG before Snow tore through Australia with seven for 40 to clinch a comfortable win. The pressure on Australia with one Test remaining was such that they replaced their captain,

TEST CRICKET

Lawry, with Ian Chappell. England won again in Sydney, a fine match in which Underwood and Illingworth excelled. Underwood took 12 more at Christchurch as England beat New Zealand by eight wickets.

An innings of 274 from Zaheer Abbas at Edgbaston in 1971 enabled Pakistan to declare on 608 for seven and England, despite an aggressive century from Knott, had to follow on against them for the first time. Impressive bowling from Asif Masood could not clinch it as a Brian Luckhurst hundred saw the hosts to safety. The series ended in a thriller at Headingley, where Pakistan were left needing 231 but excellent captaincy and bowling from Illingworth turned the screw on the final day. Pakistan fell 26 runs short to lose the rubber.

The Indian leg spinner Bhagwat Chandrasekhar perhaps had more than anyone to do with the most famous moment savoured by his country in Test cricket thus far, the triumph at the Oval that gave them their first series win in England. After a draw at Lord's, rain saved India at Old Trafford and at the Oval, England made a respectable first innings 355.

TEST CRICKET

RIGHT Dennis Lillee about to fire another missile

But the lead of 71 became largely irrelevant as Chandra ran amok, taking six for 38 in the second innings as the hosts crumbled to 101 all out. India lost six wickets in scoring the 173 they needed to win.

In 1972 Australia brought one bowler – Dennis Lillee – who was to be their most influential for a decade, and another - Bob Massie – whose influence extended largely to one performance at Lord's, where exaggerated swing confounded England to bring him 16 wickets. That, and a polished 131 from Ian Chappell's brother Greg, levelled the rubber after England had gone ahead at Old Trafford. The Headingley game, to Australia's disgust, was played on a pitch affected by a fungal disease, and Underwood ripped through them. There was some justice for Australia in proper conditions at the Oval, where both Chappells scored hundreds and Lillee took ten wickets to square the series.

Chandrasekhar continued to unstitch England in India in 1972/73, when they lost 2-1. Chandra's eight for 79 at Delhi was his Test best, and he took ten in Calcutta to clinch a low-scoring thriller. Seven more came in Madras as England were beaten again. Chandra ended the series with 35 wickets, still an Indian record. The bat dominated in Pakistan, with Dennis Amiss excelling for England. Mushtaq Mohammad had a fine series with bat and ball, while the spin trio of Norman Gifford, Pat Pocock and Jack Birkenshaw took most of the tourists' wickets.

Although New Zealand lost 2-0 in England in 1973, with Arnold bowling supremely well in conditions favouring swing, the batting of their captain, Bev Congdon, salvaged some honour. After the tourists were set 479 to win at Trent Bridge, Congdon made 176 to help his team to within just 39 runs of what would have been an historic win. He made just one fewer at Lord's before England comfortably wrapped things up at Headingley. The West Indies then won 2-0, pummelling the hosts for a glorious 652 at Lord's with both Rohan Kanhai and Sobers reaching 150. But in the Caribbean six months later Amiss followed an unavailing 174 in the first Test with an unbeaten 262 in the second, one of the great rearguard efforts that prevented the hosts from taking a 2-0 lead. Tony Greig's brief conversion to off-spin squared the series at Port of Spain with 13 wickets.

TEST CRICKET

ABOVE Mike Hendrick, Derbyshire and England fast-bowler in action

their most convincing display so far against the spinners. The series against Pakistan began with an intriguing Headingley encounter, infuriatingly washed out on day five with England, chasing 282 for victory, on 238 for six. Rain leaked under the covers at Lord's to render Underwood unplayable, but with poetic justice returned to wash that match out as well. 240 from Zaheer at the Oval set up a total of 600, but 183 from Amiss and a laboured 122 by Keith Fletcher ensured another stalemate.

By 1974/75 Lillee had recovered from a career-threatening back injury, and with Jeff Thomson he formed the opening partnership to make all England quake. Despite a counter-attacking century from Greig, the tourists were blown away at Brisbane, and a spate of injuries prompted them to recall Cowdrey who, aged nearly 43, batted as well as most. England lost at Perth before drawing an engrossing Test at the MCG. At Sydney Greg Chappell (144) and Ian Redpath (105) set Australia up for the off spin of Ashley Mallett to terminate England's Ashes tenure. The hosts won again at Adelaide and Australia's defeat back in

England cast India aside in 1974. Arnold, Chris Old, Mike Hendrick and Bob Willis routed the tourists, with England's batsmen putting up

ABOVE Mike Denness batting for Essex, his second county after Kent

Melbourne – with Lillee and Thomson both injured – was scant consolation.

England found New Zealand comparatively easy pickings. A record fourth wicket partnership of 266, with Mike Denness making 181 and Fletcher 216, gave England an innings win at Auckland. Australia won a shortened series in England in 1975 through their win at Edgbaston after being put in by Denness, who was replaced as captain by Greig. Max Walker complemented the firepower of Lillee and Thomson, and an intriguing final day at Headingley was ruined when vandals sabotaged the pitch.

THE LITTLE BOOK OF CRICKET

TEST CRICKET

ABOVE Viv Richards batting for the West Indies against his county, Somerset, in 1976

Viv Richards scored 1,710 runs for the West Indies in the 1976 calendar year, more than anyone before or since. Most came in England as his team, doubtless irritated by Greig's stated intention to make them grovel, forced England's captain to do exactly that. Richards made 232 at Nottingham and 135 at Old Trafford, where a brace of hundreds by Gordon Greenidge helped set up a 1-0 lead. After that became 2-0 at Headingley, Richards made 291 at the Oval, paving the way for Holding's matchless display of extreme pace that blew England away again.

England won 3-1 in India in 1976/77. Amiss (179) and John Lever (ten wickets) put them ahead in Delhi, and a Greig century enabled them go 2-0 up in Calcutta. Greig's batting and Lever's bowling again featured as England took an unassailable lead in Madras, before the wiles of Chandrasekhar and Bedi consoled India at Bangalore. England's next one-off encounter, at Melbourne in 1977, was played to celebrate the centenary of Anglo-Australian Tests. The hosts won a great match by 45 runs, the same result as the first Test on the same ground all those years before. It featured a never-say-die 174 by Derek Randall, which had England dreaming of victory after they were set 463. But Lillee, who had taken six for 26 as England failed to reach 100 in their first innings, had the last laugh.

Meanwhile a row had broken out between the Australian Cricket Board and a media magnate, Kerry Packer, over their refusal to sell him the television rights to cover the national team. Packer devised a tournament of his own, World Series Cricket, for which he signed up almost the entire Australian team and the cream of the crop elsewhere. Greig, who was recruiting for him during the Centenary Test, lost the England captaincy in consequence. When the ICC proposed to ban Packer players from Test cricket, the case went to the High Court, which ruled that such a ban was illegal.

Greg Chappell's Australian squad in England that summer was inevitably unsettled, and under their cerebral new captain, Mike Brearley, England won 3-0, regaining the Ashes in the fourth Test. They went ahead at Old Trafford, primarily through Bob Woolmer's bat and the bowling of Underwood, and at Trent Bridge they were rescued from the perils of 82 for five by the recalled Boycott and Knott, who made his best Test score of 135. It was a match-winning partnership, and Boycott reached his hundredth first-class hundred in the series-clinching sequel on his home ground of Headingley, eventually reaching 191 to ensure there was no way back for Australia.

The tenor for a dull series in Pakistan in 1977/78 was set in Lahore by Mudassar Nazar, who took nine hours and 17 minutes to make the slowest-ever Test century. At Hyderabad Haroon Rashid briefly raised the tone,

ABOVE Derek Randall doffs his cap to Dennis Lillee after ducking a bouncer during the Centenary Test at the MCG in 1977

TEST CRICKET

hitting six sixes in his 108, and England were sternly tested, not for the last time, by the leg spin of Abdul Qadir. They were left needing 344 but Boycott and Brearley shared a draw-ensuring stand of 185 in nearly five and a half hours. In Karachi England took the best part of two days to make 266, amid several hold-ups as bored members of the crowd threw oranges on to the outfield. Phil Edmonds managed a Test-best seven for 66 on the way to another stultifying draw.

England moved on to New Zealand, where Richard Hadlee showed his maturity on an uneven surface in Wellington, with ten wickets as his team beat England at last. The visitors were decimated for just 64 in their second innings, but bounced back at Christchurch through Ian Botham. The young Somerset all-rounder scored a century, took eight wickets and is reported to have deliberately run out Boycott, whose slow scoring was jeopardising his team's eventual win.

The deadlock with Pakistan was finally broken in England's favour later that year. Incisive bowling at Edgbaston from Old dismissed Pakistan for 164 and hundreds from

Clive Radley and Botham put England 288 in front, more than enough for an innings win which they repeated at Lord's thanks almost entirely to Botham. He followed a run-a-ball century with eight for 34, his best Test figures, as the tourists were routed in less than 13 hours. A maiden hundred at the Oval by David Gower set England on the path to another 3-0 win over New Zealand, before Botham and Willis completed the rout.

Due to the Packer intrusion, the sides contesting the 1978/79 Ashes series, particularly Australia's, were not fully representative. Brearley's team was much too strong, winning 5-1. Following the wind-up of World Series Cricket the following season, Australia were boosted by the return of players like Greg Chappell, Rod Marsh and Lillee and won 3-0.

1979 signalled the decline of India's spin attack and the emergence of Kapil Dev, their great all-rounder. Although he took five wickets at Edgbaston, no one else struck and England, thanks primarily to a silken, unbeaten double century from Gower, declared on 633 for five. The innings victory that ensued was the only result of a rubber in which Dilip Vengsarkar scored the first of his three hundreds at Lord's, and a great innings at the Oval of 221 from Sunil Gavaskar brought India within a tantalising nine runs of the 438 they had been set by Brearley's declaration.

ABOVE Richard Hadlee salutes the crowd

LEFT Outstanding England captain Mike Brearley

ABOVE Graham Gooch gets his first century for England on the first day of the second Test against the West Indies at Lord's in 1980

India fell foul of Botham in the Jubilee Test of 1980. The all-rounder scored 114 and took 13 wickets as England won by 10 wickets. Wicket-keeper Bob Taylor took ten catches, a world record at the time. Botham's brief tenure as England's captain then began with a 1-0 defeat, with Malcolm Marshall now in the West Indies attack and Graham Gooch playing the first of several fine knocks against them, 123 at Lord's. Gooch was one of the few to make an impression the following winter on a tour blighted by the death of England's assistant manager Ken Barrington. West Indies won the series 2-0.

One of the great Ashes contests was won by England in 1981. Australia went one up at Trent Bridge through Lillee and Terry Alderman, and after a Lord's draw Botham's resignation as England's captain paved the way back for his old mentor, Brearley. The nearest thing to a miracle that cricket can have seen ensued. At Headingley Botham's unbeaten 149 after England followed on gave Australia an unexpected victory target of 130 that Willis, bowling at great pace, prevented then from reaching. At Edgbaston lightning struck twice; Australia needed 151 and Botham, rushing in like England's talisman of old, took five wickets for one run in 25 balls and England were ahead.

At Old Trafford he played an innings of 118 that surpassed even his

TEST CRICKET

Headingley knock in quality, effectively clinching one of the most enthralling Ashes contests. It came off just 102 balls and included six sixes, one of which, off Dennis Lillee, he seemed to swat off his eyebrows. Despite centuries from Yallop and Border, the target of 506 was beyond Australia. The final match at the Oval was drawn, despite the efforts of Lillee, who took 11 more wickets.

There was nothing spellbinding about the cricket in India the following winter. After Kapil Dev and Madan Lal had bowled the hosts to victory in the first Test in Bombay, they defended dourly for the rest of the six-match series, ensuring five excruciating draws before England went on to win their inaugural Test against Sri Lanka. Botham and Willis were too much for India's batsman, with the exception of Vengsarkar who made a second innings 157, and Kapil Dev (130 in the match), at Lord's in 1982. England's seven-wicket win preceded draws at Old Trafford and the Oval, where Botham reached his best Test score of 208.

England again beat Pakistan in the second half of the summer. At Edgbaston, Imran Khan took seven

ABOVE Dennis Lillee with the classical fast bowler's action

TEST CRICKET

wickets as England were dismissed for 272, but a second innings century from Derek Randall left the tourists needing 313, too many thanks to the bowling of Botham and Willis. The latter was injured for the Lord's Test and England missed him, as Mohsin Khan hit an elegant double century. The hosts followed on after problems with Qadir and capitulated to the medium pace of Mudassar. But England clinched matters in a classic at Headingley; the returning Willis helped bowl the tourists out for 275 and 199, and the hosts needed just 219 for victory. They were almost foiled by the indomitable Imran and Mudassar before inching home by three wickets.

In 1982/83 Greg Chappell fulfilled his ambition to lead an Ashes-winning Australian team. England, shorn of several players who had joined an unofficial tour of South Africa, lost in Brisbane and at Adelaide where Chappell scored a century for Thomson, Rodney Hogg and Geoff Lawson to complete the job. The game at the MCG became one of Test cricket's tensest. Australia, set 292 to win, looked out of it when Thomson joined Allan Border at 218 for nine. They had moved

TEST CRICKET

to within four runs of a sensational win when Botham found an edge from Thomson which a nervous Chris Tavare at second slip cold only parry, Geoff Miller holding the rebound.

New Zealand had Lance Cairns to thank for their first victory in England; after his team went 1-0 down at the Oval Cairns took seven for 74 at Headingley as England were bowled out for 225. Not even another hundred by Gower and sustained hostility from Willis could prevent New Zealand reaching the 103-run victory target. They nonetheless lost the rubber 3-1 but took revenge the following winter. England were turned over at Christchurch, replying to 307 with just 82 and 93. Hadlee took eight of the wickets, and a draw at Auckland ensured the hosts' first-ever series win against England.

Pakistan, without an injured Imran, could thank Abdul Qadir, who took eight wickets in the first Test in Karachi, for their first home win over England. There were some heart-fluttering moments as they lost seven wickets reaching the small target of 65. By now the West Indies were the dominant force in world cricket, a fact emphasised during their tour of England in 1984, the year of the first 'blackwash'. Greenidge scored two double centuries and only Allan Lamb provided any significant

LEFT India's Kapil Dev in action for Northamptonshire

BELOW Bob Willis wins an appeal for lbw against Greg Chappell during the fifth Ashes Test in Sydney at Sydney in 1983

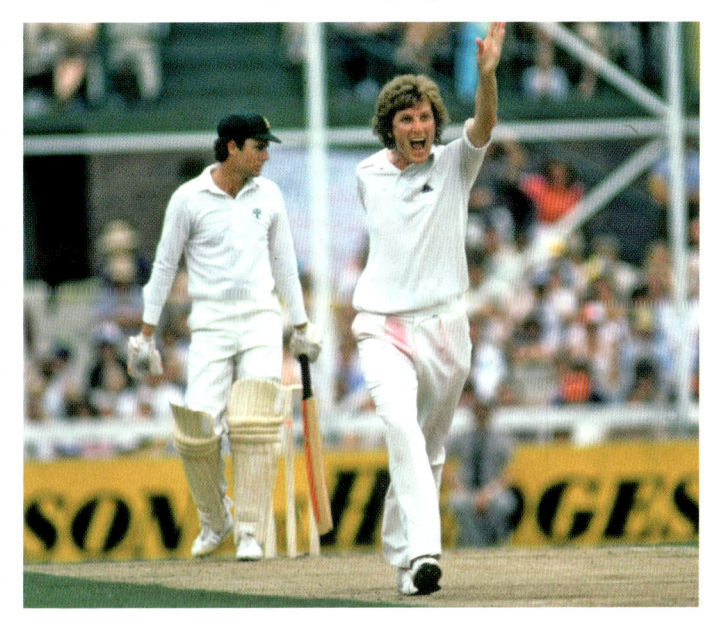

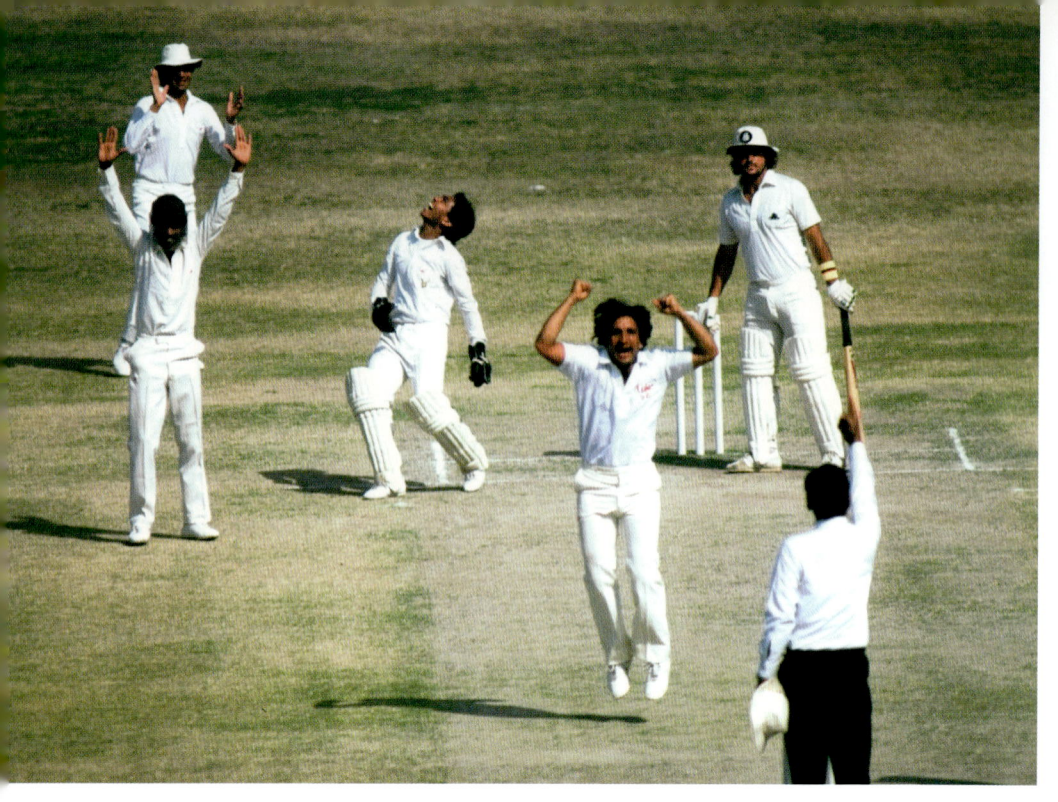

ABOVE Abdul Qadir of Pakistan celebrates after he captures the vital wicket of Allan Lamb of England during the first Test in Karachi in 1984

riposte, with three hundreds, as England were pulverised 5-0, a humiliation repeated in the Caribbean 18 months later. Nor could England manage to beat Sri Lanka in the final Test of the summer.

The 1984/85 tour of India started unpropitiously. Two assassinations – of the prime minister, Indira Gandhi, and the British deputy high commissioner Percy Norris – put the tour into doubt and when the first Test went ahead England were hardly in the right frame of mind, losing by eight wickets. They won by the same margin in Delhi, aided by Tim Robinson's 160 and the spin of Pocock and Edmonds. Double centuries for Graeme Fowler and Mike Gatting in

TEST CRICKET

Madras, and 11 wickets for Neil Foster, ensured a 2-1 triumph for England.

1985 was the last Ashes summer to savour in England for 20 years. 175 from Tim Robinson and the bowling of Botham and Emburey put England ahead at Headingley, but at Lord's Craig McDermott and Bob Holland ensured full value from a tenacious 196 from Border and the series was level. Edgbaston was a dream game for Richard Ellison, who took ten wickets, and one of Gower's finest Test knocks (215), allied to hundreds from Robinson and Gatting to ensure England only needed to bat once. At the Oval Gooch (196) and Gower (157) provided one of Test cricket's spectacular partnerships, and Ellison again shone with the ball as Australia, who had sorely missed Alderman, surrendered the urn.

India's visit to England in 1986 was a successful one. Spineless batting by the hosts (Gooch and Derek Pringle excepted) and the now customary Lord's ton for Vengsarkar put the visitors one up, then two at Headingley where Vengsarkar managed another. New Zealand's Test graduation was then confirmed as they took a rubber in England for the first time. Hadlee was again pivotal, with ten wickets at Nottingham while a century from the off-spinner John Bracewell, batting at

ABOVE Phil DeFreitas in appealling pose

TEST CRICKET

number eight, ensured a straightforward victory target.

England retained the Ashes in Australia in 1986/87. Botham (138) put England in charge at Brisbane before Graham Dilley took five wickets as Australia were forced to follow on, the job being completed by Emburey and Phil DeFreitas. After two draws the Ashes were secured at the MCG, a century from Chris Broad bolstering England after Botham and Gladstone Small had dismissed the hosts for 141. The spin of Emburey and Edmonds finished them off, although they made it 2-1 at Sydney.

The critical game with Pakistan in 1987 was at Headingley where Imran was key. England were dismissed for 136 and 99 from Salim Malik gave Pakistan a lead of 217. Imran's seven second-innings wickets ensured that there was no need for his team to bat again. After 13 wickets from Qadir put Pakistan 1-0 up in Lahore the next winter, Gatting was involved in an unholy row in Faisalabad after the umpire Shakoor Rana accused him of cheating in the field. Six hours were lost while Gatting was forced to apologise, a delay that may well have saved

TEST CRICKET

the game for Pakistan. It was the most heated of several umpiring disputes between the two sides. The Faisalabad and Karachi Tests were both drawn despite the efforts of Qadir, who took an astonishing 30 wickets in an ill-tempered series. England, who went on to draw all three Tests in New Zealand, would not tour Pakistan again for 13 years.

In 1988 England avoided a third successive West Indies blackwash by the narrowest of margins, 4-0 with one Test drawn. By then Marshall was leading an attack including Joel Garner's natural successor, the giant Antiguan Curtly Ambrose. England did record their first home win over

LEFT Ian Botham hooks another six on his way to 118 against Australia at Old Trafford in 1981

BELOW Mike Gatting and Peter Lush argue with controversial umpire Shakoor Rana (left), during England's tour of Pakistan, 1987

ABOVE Australia celebrate retaining the Ashes at Old Trafford in 1989

Sri Lanka at the end of the summer, and Gooch again impressed in the Caribbean in 1989/90 until his hand was broken by a delivery from Ezra Moseley. Another ton from Lamb enabled England to lead 1-0 after the first Test, and the eventual 2-1 victory for the hosts seemed a comparatively respectable scoreline.

In 1989 Alderman passed the 40-wicket mark in an Ashes series for the second time. At Leeds and Headingley he struck 19 times, and after Steve Waugh had begun in England with 177

TEST CRICKET

Geoff Marsh (138). The Ashes would not return to England for 16 years.

The importance of Hadlee to New Zealand's success was shown by the decline that followed his retirement, after yet another impressive display in England in 1990. He ended with a five-wicket haul – his 36th in Tests – on his English home ground of Trent Bridge. 154 from Gooch helped clinch the rubber at Edgbaston, and at Lord's against India he made a monumental 333 as England amassed 653 for four. Mohammad Azharuddin made an eye-catching 121 before Kapil Dev neatly avoided the follow-on with four consecutive sixes off Eddie Hemmings. Gooch's second innings 123 completed the highest individual aggregate in a Test before he declared leaving India needing 472, which was well beyond them.

Alderman continued to torment England Down Under in 1990/91, bowling Australia to victory with eight wickets in the opener in Brisbane. Despite a Gower century they went two up at the MCG as the tall left armer Bruce Reid enjoyed his finest hour with 13 wickets. Australia had already retained the Ashes by the last match at

and 152, Australia were two up. They eventually made it 4-0, winning at Old Trafford despite Robin Smith (143) and Jack Russell (128), and at Trent Bridge where Alderman took seven more scalps after a huge opening stand of 329 between Mark Taylor (219) and

TEST CRICKET

the WACA, where Craig McDermott struck ten times, enabling Australia to take the series 3-0.

Gooch's finest hour came the following summer, amid signs that the West Indies' glorious era was behind them. At Headingley he carried his bat for a match-winning 154 in England's second innings, in adverse conditions against Marshall, Ambrose, Walsh and Patrick Patterson. Although the West Indies won at Nottingham and Birmingham England managed, thanks in part to Robin Smith with the bat and Phil Tufnell with the ball, to square an engaging rubber two-all at the Oval. Against Sri Lanka 174 from Gooch converted England's slight advantage into an impregnable one and Phil Tufnell spun the hosts to victory.

England were too strong for New Zealand in 1991/92, with Gooch and Alec Stewart the batting stars, and Imran had retired by the time Pakistan toured England the following summer. The emerging Wasim Akram and Waqar Younis dominated an enthralling game at Lord's, and with Pakistan wobbling in pursuit of just 138 to win, Wasim batted them to victory. A fine opening stand between

TEST CRICKET

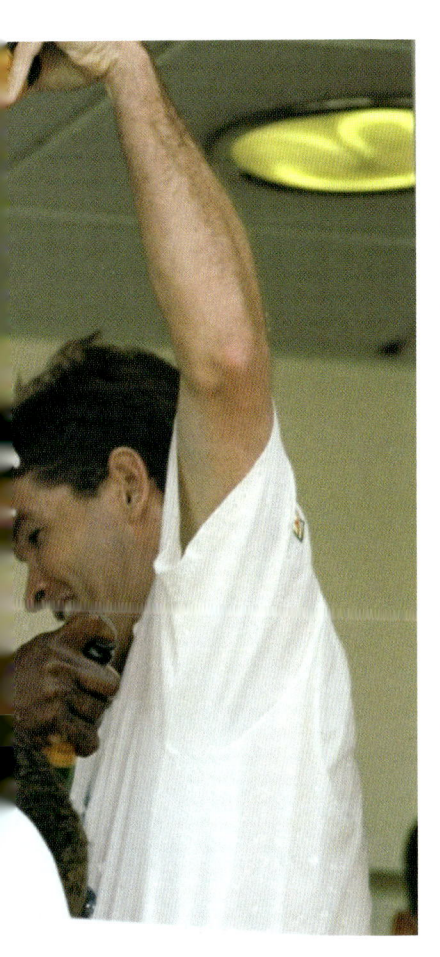

Gooch and Mike Atherton enabled England to hit back at Headingley but Pakistan, with Wasim and Waqar again influential, comfortably took the series 2-1 at the Oval.

India swept England aside in 1992/93. 182 from Azharuddin and six wickets for the leg spinner Anil Kumble put them ahead in Calcutta, and England had no answer to him, or to the hosts' 560 for six, in Madras. Despite 178 from Graeme Hick, another innings defeat ensured India's first-ever clean sweep. England moved on to Sri Lanka, where a spin bowler had emerged upon whom his team's fortunes were to depend for well over a decade. Muttiah Muralitharan's influence on his first match against England was limited – he took five wickets – by comparison with what was to follow. The tourists surrendered a lead of 91 despite a first-innings century from Robin Smith, and eight wickets for another spinner, Jayananda Warnaweera, propelled Sri Lanka to their first win over England.

Meanwhile Allan Border had now turned Australia into a side strong enough to beat even the West Indies, and in England in 1993 they beat much weaker opposition 4-1. The 'ball of the

LEFT Graeme Hick pours champagne over Devon Malcolm after his nine second innings wickets helped England beat South Africa at the Oval, 1994

TEST CRICKET

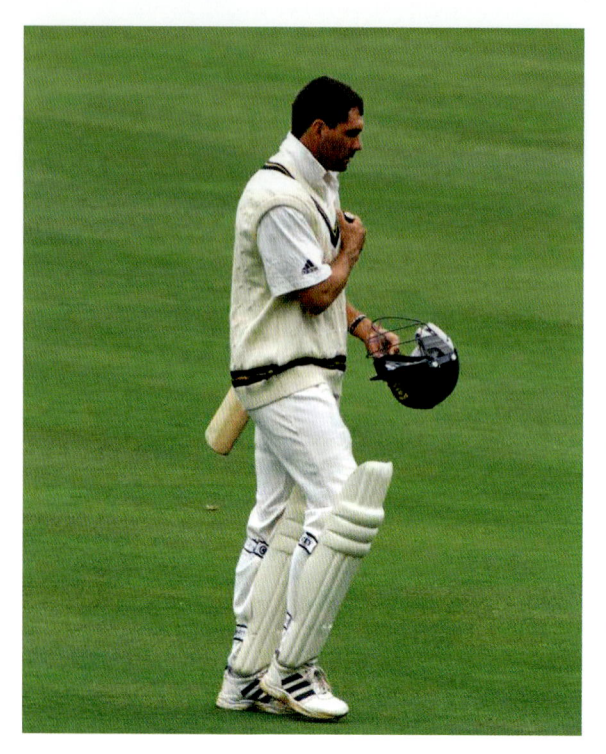

ABOVE Hansie Cronje of South Africa returns to the pavilion after scoring 0 during the fifth Test against England, 2000

Australia went one up. Centuries from Taylor, Michael Slater and David Boon set up an innings win as Warne prospered again at Lord's, with only Mike Atherton providing significant resistance. England were routed at Headingley and as was to become something of a habit, they won the final Test with the Ashes already decided.

Brian Lara's world record 375 at Antigua came at the end of a series against England that was already secure for the West Indies in 1993/94. A Gooch double century then combined with the bowling of Phil DeFreitas to set up England's decisive win over New Zealand at Nottingham. One of their great batsmen, Martin Crowe, ended on the losing side despite scoring 380 runs in the three-match series. England then met the re-admitted South Africa, in the drawn series of 1994 memorable for Devon Malcolm's demolition of the tourists at the Oval with nine for 57.

The Australian pairing of Slater (176) and Steve Waugh's twin brother Mark (140) set England off on the wrong foot again at the 'Gabba in 1994/95, McDermott and Warne finishing them off as they were to do

century' set the tone at Old Trafford as Shane Warne, bowling his first delivery in Ashes cricket, produced a perfect leg break that turned sharply from outside Mike Gatting's leg stump to hit the top of the off. Warne took eight wickets as

again at the MCG, putting Australia 2-0 up. A draw in Sydney was enough to secure the Ashes for Australia, although England did manage to win at Adelaide, with Gatting making his final Test century and Malcolm taking seven wickets. The baggy green supremacy was confirmed in Perth, where Glenn McGrath took three wickets in each innings.

Atherton's England could not manage victory over the West Indies in 1995, although Dominic Cork twice levelled the series with seven for 43 on debut at Lord's, then a hat-trick at Old Trafford after England had again gone behind on a fast bowler-friendly pitch at Edgbaston. Allan Donald and Shaun Pollock then secured the 1995/96 rubber in South Africa by their efforts in the final Test in Cape Town. It followed a famous English escape, as Atherton made an unbeaten 185 in the second Test at Johannesburg, sharing an unbroken partnership of 119 in four and a half hours with Russell that deprived the hosts of apparently certain victory. Russell also took 11 catches behind the stumps in the match, still a world record.

The first Test against India in 1996 was key, played at Edgbaston and featuring a crucial 128 from Nasser Hussain. A century from Tendulkar aside, India's batsmen had no answer to England's seamers and an eight-wicket win was enough to secure the rubber. But England were no match for Pakistan, with Wasim, now a connoisseur of swing, and Waqar, master of the toe crusher, backed up by the inex-

ABOVE Shaun Pollock celebrates dismissing Graeme Hick for 141 in the first Test at Centurion Park, 1995

THE LITTLE BOOK OF CRICKET **95**

ABOVE Mike Atherton and Jack Russell celebrate after drawing the second Test against South Africa in Johannesburg, 1995

RIGHT Allan Donald bowling at his best for South Africa against England at Trent Bridge in 1998

haustible leg-spinner Mushtaq Ahmed. The tourists won at Lord's after a majestic 148 from Inzamam-ul-Haq, and clinched it 2-0 at the Oval with a big hundred from Saeed Anwar and an unbeaten one from Malik.

England's first two Tests against Zimbabwe were in 1996/97. At Bulawayo, they failed by one run to force a win after a century for Andy Flower, upon whom Zimbabwe depended so heavily. Another key figure, Heath Streak, took four wickets in Harare and the hosts led before a Stewart ton, and a wet outfield that prevented play on the final day, settled English nerves. The bowling of Darren Gough and Andrew Caddick inspired England in New Zealand, while Atherton imposed himself at the crease, with 94 and 118 at Christchurch to ensure a 2-0 series win.

Australia were given a shock at Edgbaston in 1997, bowled out for 118 by Gough and Caddick before Hussain (207) and Graham Thorpe (138) added 288 for the fourth wicket, an England record against Australia. England went one up, but at Old Trafford it was business as usual. Two centuries for Steve Waugh and 16 wickets for McGrath and Warne outclassed the hosts, while Jason Gillespie unstitched them at Leeds, where Matthew Elliott made 199. Monotonously 2-1 became 3-1 at Edgbaston before the spin of Tufnell

TEST CRICKET

allied to Caddick's pace gave England victory at the Oval.

England again lost in the Caribbean in 1997/98, despite the bowling efforts of Angus Fraser, whose 20 wickets in two Trinidad Tests (the first in Jamaica was abandoned due to an unsafe pitch) saw England first fall narrowly short and then win, only to go down ultimately by three matches to one.

Donald and Atherton provided one of Test cricket's red-toothed passages of play at Trent Bridge during South Africa's visit in 1998. Donald was furious after Atherton refused to walk for what the bowler considered to be a gloved catch to the wicket-keeper, Mark Boucher. Atherton held firm and a crucial match was won by England, who went on to take the rubber 2-1. But they fell foul of Muralitharan against Sri Lanka at the Oval. The hosts made 445 after being put in by Ranatunga, John Crawley making an unbeaten 156 and Hick 107. But Jayasuriya (213) and Aravinda de Silva (152) left England wallowing in their wake. Murali, having already reaped seven wickets in the first innings, took nine in the second as the home side were dismissed for 181.

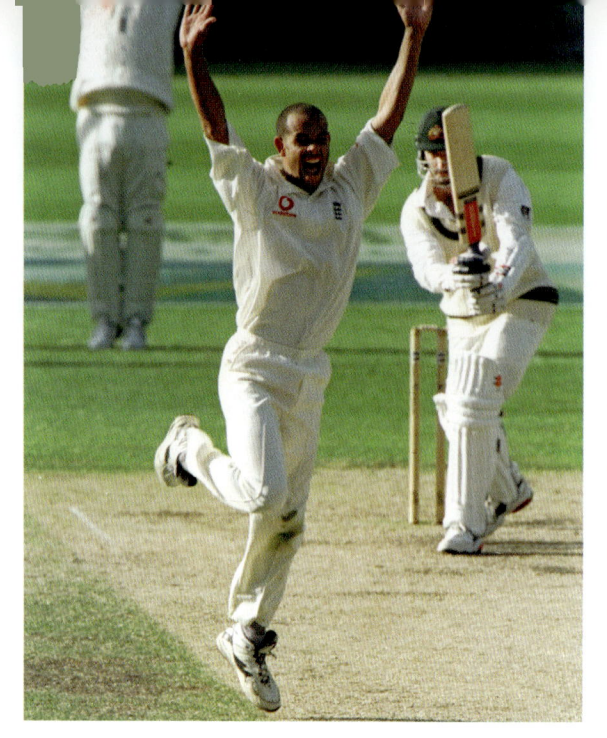

ABOVE Dean Headley takes the wicket of Damien Fleming during the fourth Ashes Test in Melbourne, 1998

RIGHT Ashley Giles celebrates a wicket against India in the 2001/02 series

Although England drew the 1998/99 opener in Brisbane, the ensuing tale was depressingly familiar. McGrath, Gillespie and now Damien Fleming harassed their batsmen to extinction at Perth, and 179 from Justin Langer led the way at Adelaide before McGrath and Fleming put Australia two up and the urn beyond reach again. Dean Headley enjoyed his moment in the sun at the MCG. Centuries from Alec Stewart and Steve Waugh dominated the early stages, but with Australia needing just 175 to win Headley scythed through them with six for 60. In Sydney England were spun out by Stuart MacGill.

In 1999 New Zealand met an England side in such disarray that it was labelled the worst in the world. Although a remarkable, unbeaten 99 by nightwatchman Alex Tudor ensured victory at Edgbaston, England were not to win again. They went down at Lord's primarily thanks to the batting of Matt Horne and the bowling of Chris Cairns, who showed his all-round qualities at The Oval as New Zealand polished the hosts off.

South Africa won 2-1 on England's next tour in 1999/2000, although the tourists' one win at Centurion was contrived. The home captain, Hansie Cronje, was initially given the credit for making a match of it with a bold declaration, but his true motive became apparent when it emerged that he had received 53,000 rand and a leather jacket for his wife from a bookmaker. Cronje was the arch villain in cricket's match-fixing scandal, banned for life for encouraging members of his team to under-perform. He was killed in a plane crash in 2002.

England's first home Test against Zimbabwe, at Lord's in 2000, produced a more convincing display. Centuries from Stewart and Hick ensured that they only needed to bat once, as the tourists were swept aside by Gough, Caddick and Ed Giddins. Nonetheless when England went down by an innings to the West Indies, things did not look good for the hosts. However they won a low-scoring thriller at Lord's, and after Stewart had scored a century in his 100th Test at Old Trafford, Gough and Caddick sent the tourists hurtling to an almost unbelievable two-day defeat at Headingley. An emphatic win at The Oval returned the Wisden Trophy to England for the first time since 1969.

England finally returned to Pakistan in 2000/01 and the series lacked the acrimony of the previous one. The bat dominated in Lahore and Faisalabad, where results were never likely, and a similar outcome seemed probable in Karachi. But disciplined bowling, particularly from Gough and Ashley Giles, chiselled away at Pakistan and suddenly England needed only 176 to win.

ABOVE A hundred for Craig White against India in Ahmedabad in 2001

rubber in Pakistan since 1961 and the hosts' first-ever defeat in Karachi.

England maintained the winning habit in Sri Lanka despite going 1-0 down at Galle. A welcome return to form for the captain, Hussain, helped his team to a 90-run lead in Kandy, and eight wickets for the ebullient Gough left England needing 161. Thorpe shepherded them to victory by three wickets before playing one of the matches of his life in Colombo. He made 113 to keep England on terms, and after Gough, Caddick and Giles had shot the hosts out for 81 he fought off cramp and dehydration to see England to another tight win.

Just two Tests were played between England and Pakistan the following summer, Thorpe top-scoring for England at Lord's before Gough and Caddick tore through Pakistan for what was effectively a three-day innings win. Centuries from Thorpe and Michael Vaughan at Old Trafford kept the hosts in contention, but 199 runs in the match from Inzamam-ul-Haq left England with a stiff target of 370, of which they fell more then 100 short.

Thorpe and Hick took them close amid blatant time wasting by Pakistan. The gathering gloom added to the drama as with 15 balls to spare England completed an historic win, their first in a

Improving though England were, they were still no match for Australia.

TEST CRICKET

At Edgbaston they witnessed the might of Adam Gilchrist, who made 152 off just 143 balls before McGrath, Gillespie and Warne polished the hosts off. Dropped catches compounded England's woes at Lord's, where McGrath was rampant again. Australia made sure of the Ashes at Trent Bridge, where the game ended on the third afternoon. The consolation win came at Headingley, where Butcher made 173 after a sporting declaration from Gilchrist, leading Australia after Steve Waugh had injured a calf. Such was the Australian captain's toughness that he returned to hobble his way to 157 at the Oval, where Warne took 11 wickets and the hosts were outplayed again.

In India in 2001/02, England fatally went 1-0 behind in the first Test in Mohali, tormented by Kumble and Harbhajan Singh. A century from Craig White could not force a result in Ahmedabad, and the match at Bangalore was ruined by rain. But in New Zealand later that winter, England won a fantastic Test at Christchurch. Hussain bonded their first innings 228 with a century, before Thorpe (200) and Andrew Flintoff (137) left the hosts needing 550 for victory. Astoundingly they got within 99 runs as Nathan Astle made 222 off just 168 balls. New Zealand squared matters at Auckland thanks to Daryl Tuffey, who took nine wickets, and 114 runs in the

BELOW Marcus Trescothick celebrates his double century during the fifth Test against South Africa at the Oval, 2003

TEST CRICKET

RIGHT Jacques Kallis batting for South Africa against England in Durban, 2004

the tourists up at Lord's where England followed on, but consistent batting let them out of jail. They made Sri Lanka pay at Edgbaston, where Marcus Trescothick and Thorpe imposed themselves before a five-wicket haul for Matthew Hoggard completed an innings win. England almost ran out of time at Old Trafford, but they bowled Sri Lanka out twice with just six overs remaining and 50 runs needed. Trescothick and Vaughan knocked them off with an over in hand.

England went one up against India after Hussain made 155 at Lord's. Hundreds from Butcher and John Crawley piled on the pressure after India fell for 228, and Ajit Agarkar's century was in vain. Vaughan (197) dominated the drawn second Test at Trent Bridge, but at Headingley Tendulkar made 193 and Dravid 148, while the captain, Ganguly, contributed 128 before declaring on 628

match from Chris Harris.

England maintained their superiority over Sri Lanka in 2002. Another big innings from Atapattu and a ton from Mahela Jayawardene looked to have set

TEST CRICKET

for eight. England battled, but were ultimately forced to bow. After another sublime effort at the Oval from Vaughan, who fell just five short of 200, Dravid passed the landmark before rain washed out what had promised to be an intriguing last day of the series.

Hussain's decision to put Australia in at the 'Gabba at the start of the 2002/03 series opened another door to Ashes destruction. Matthew Hayden made 197 and Ricky Ponting 123, and Simon Jones, who had taken an early wicket, sustained a knee injury in the field that ruled him out of the series. McGrath, Gillespie and Warne again ensured the prey was not released. At Adelaide 177 from Vaughan only delayed the inevitable; 154 from Ponting and more wickets for McGrath put Australia two up. The

ABOVE The pace quartet of Hoggard, Harmison, Flintoff and Jones that did so much to win the Ashes in 2005

THE LITTLE BOOK OF CRICKET **103**

TEST CRICKET

ABOVE Australian players Glenn McGrath (L), Ricky Ponting (2/L), Jason Gillespie (C), Michael Kasprowicz (2/R) and Shane Warne (R) celebrate as Australia demolished New Zealand on the fourth day of the first Test in Brisbane, 2004

pacy Brett Lee joined the party at Perth, as England were humbled by an innings again. But for the class of Vaughan, who made 145, they would have been again at Melbourne, where the margin of defeat was just five wickets. With the Ashes party over England won a fine match at the SCG. Vaughan topped his previous fine knocks with 183 and Australia were bowled out by Caddick.

Zimbabwe found England far too strong in 2003, going down by an innings both at Lord's and Chester-le-Street. England and South Africa then contested another compelling series. The tourists could not win it despite twice going ahead, and in the final Test at the Oval England retrieved an apparently lost cause. The visitors posted a seemingly impregnable 484 but England, sustained by Trescothick and Thorpe and fuelled by Flintoff, declared on 604 for nine. Confounded, South Africa subsided for 229 and England won by nine wickets.

England had to work hard to win their first Test against Bangladesh in Dhaka in 2003/04. Hoggard and Stephen Harmison were the destructive bowlers, but the hosts still managed to set a target of 164, which was reached thanks to a fluent, unbeaten 81 from Vaughan. The gap was wider in Chittagong, where Hussain (76 and 95) helped ensure a 329-run win.

Meanwhile Muralitharan awaited England's return to his favourite Galle dustbowl, where he all but pulled off another win. His seven first innings wickets gave the hosts a lead but England, set 323 to win, held on through their last-wicket pair of Giles and Hoggard. At Kandy a century from Vaughan enabled the tourists to survive more comfortably, with Muralitharan and the left-arm seamer Chaminda Vaas the main threats. The pressure finally told in Colombo, where Sri Lanka responded to an inadequate 265 with 628. Four more strikes from Murali forced England to surrender the rubber.

Nonetheless, by the time England arrived in the Caribbean they were firm favourites. An x-rated second innings display by the hosts in Jamaica – where they were bowled out for 47 as Harmison took a stunning seven for 12 – did nothing to contradict

ABOVE The England team celebrate after beating Zimbabwe on the third day of the second Test, 2003

TEST CRICKET

ABOVE Andrew Strauss during his Test debut hundred at Lord's against New Zealand in 2004

RIGHT Ashley Giles celebrates catching Australian Simon Katich during the Old Trafford Test of 2005

the bookies' assessment. The Trinidad Test went the same way, and a century from Thorpe combined with a Hoggard hat-trick to hand England the series in Barbados. Although Lara regained the world batting record with his unbeaten 400 at Antigua, there was no disguising the disparity between the teams.

England's progress was confirmed with a comprehensive home win over New Zealand in 2004. A magnificent debut for Andrew Strauss (112 and 83) at Lord's culminated in a match-winning hundred for Hussain after which he bowed out of Test cricket. Battle though New Zealand did, England's four-man pace attack was too strong for them. They were trounced at Leeds, where Trescothick founded a huge England total, and lost more narrowly at the Oval despite hundreds from Stephen Fleming and Scott Styris, as Thorpe saw England home with a second innings century. England trounced the West Indies 4-0 later in the summer, their balance assisted immeasurably by the emergence of Flintoff as a world-class all-rounder.

The pace quartet of Flintoff, Hoggard, Harmison and Jones played a major role in England's 2-1 win in the 2004/05 series in South Africa. Jacques Kallis shone for South Africa, but failed in the crucial fourth Test in Johannesburg, where hundreds from Strauss and Trescothick paved the way for an England triumph. Bangladesh were then outclassed on their first visit to England, as the home pace attack swept away their batsman.

The 2005 Ashes series began promisingly at Lord's as Australia were bowled out for 190, Harmison taking five wickets. But by the end of day one McGrath had reduced England to 92 for seven. Improved batting in Australia's second innings allowed Warne and McGrath to consign England to defeat. But at Edgbaston, while Australia were warming up in the outfield, McGrath contrived to turn his ankle on a stray ball. Ponting then put England in and aggressive batting, with Trescothick to the fore, and fiery bowling from Flintoff gave them a lead. Warne and Lee bowled well to keep Australia's target down to 282, but at 175 for eight they seemed beaten. However Lee, first with Warne and then with Mike Kasprowicz, edged Australia nearer until, with just three needed, Kasprowicz gloved Harmison to wicket-keeper Geraint Jones and England had drawn level.

It was to prove the turning point of an astonishing series. Two more great Tests followed, first at Old Trafford, where Vaughan made 166 before Simon Jones took six wickets, some with reverse swing, to put Australia 142 behind. But for rain on day three they

TEST CRICKET

RIGHT Andrew Flintoff starts the celebrations after England's Ashes success of 2005

would surely have lost; in fact they were saved by 156 from Ponting. At Trent Bridge it was the bat of Flintoff that put England in control, while Australia, never at ease with Hoggard, Harmison, Flintoff and Jones, were forced to follow on for the first time since 1988. England were left needing 129 and Warne almost managed to stop them. Seven wickets fell to him and Lee before Giles and Hoggard saw England past the post.

Strauss and Flintoff excelled as England reached 373 at the Oval and Australia, after centuries from Langer and Hayden, were forced by magnificent bowling from Flintoff and Hoggard to surrender a small lead. But on day five the old firm of Warne and McGrath reduced England to 126 for five. Enter Kevin Pietersen, who was dropped twice on the way to 15 before putting the issue beyond doubt. He hit seven sixes in a display of extraordinary aggression before, on 158 and with the Ashes effectively regained by England, he was bowled by McGrath. The crowd, aided and abetted by spectators on every available rooftop, were ecstatic. It was surely the greatest Ashes series in living memory; quite possibly, it was the greatest ever.

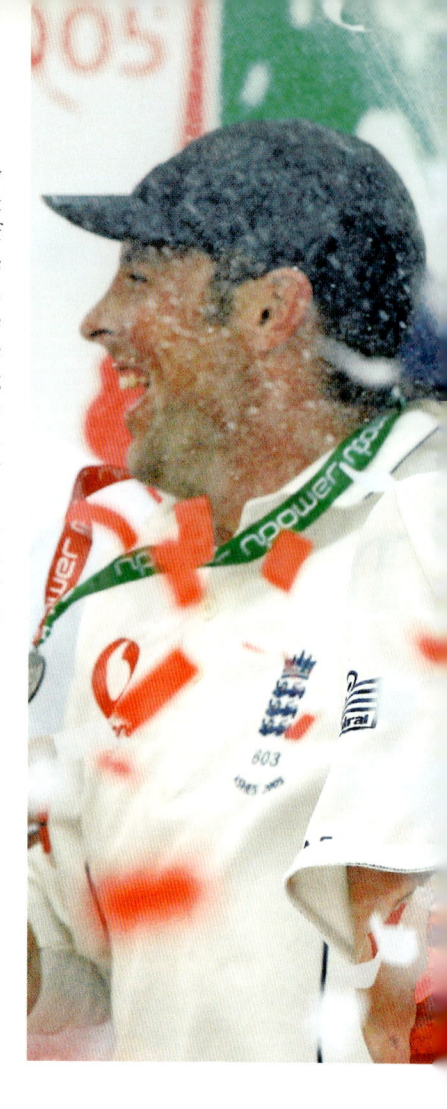

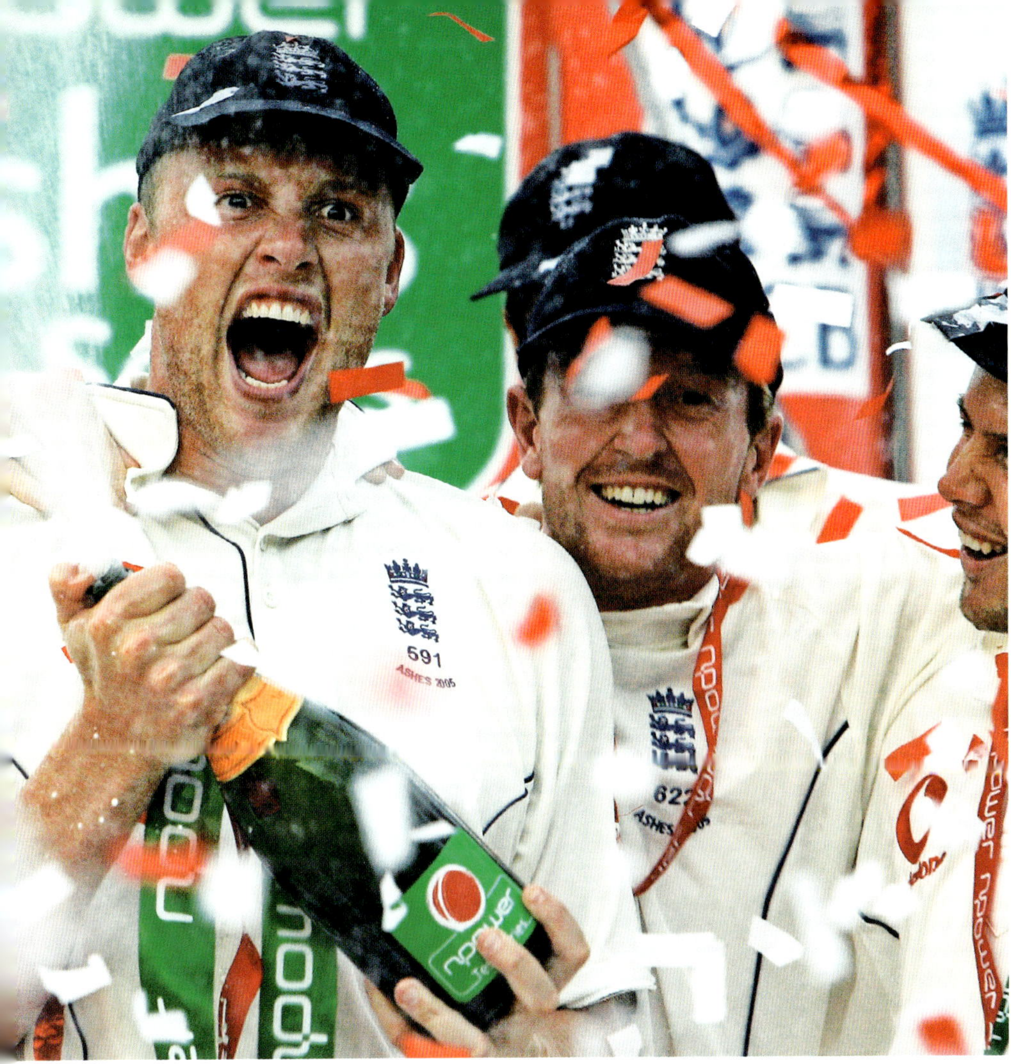
591
ASHES 2005

Chapter 4

The Players

RIGHT 'The Doctor', W. G. Grace

CONSTRAINTS OF SPACE IN SUCH a book as this prevent the detailed study of players from every country and all time, so the spotlight is on English players of modern era. That could be said to start in 1865 when W.G. Grace made his first-class debut. The likes of Parr and Lillywhite, representatives of a previous time, were still playing, but Grace was the bridge between the old and modern eras and could be said to have defined the new age of cricket.

From the time he was 18 and scored an unbeaten 224 for England against Surrey at the Oval, Grace dominated English cricket for four decades. The "Champion" scored over 54,000 first-class runs at an average a shade under 40. His round-arm bowling accounted for more than 2,800 wickets and he held over 870 catches. Grace stood out on his own, but others made their mark in his time. A.C. MacLaren was a despotic captain who even outscored WG to establish an individual batting record. Grace had made 344 in 1876 playing for MCC against Kent at Canterbury, but in 1895 MacLaren made 424 for Lancashire against Somerset at Taunton.

Between 1896 and 1902 England could boast in their number the man who was to become Colonel His Highness Shri Sir Ranjithsinji Vibhaji, Maharajah Jam Saheb of Nawanag, but who was better known as simply Ranji. He was a prince among batsman, not merely on account of the runs he accumulated, but the way he scored them.

England produced several notable bowlers in this era, like Bobby Peel who was the first Englishman to take 100 Test wickets, an effort that he matched with the extent of his celebrations. He was dismissed by Yorkshire for taking the field while under the influence and when, as the story goes, he relieved himself against the sightscreen, his captain, Lord Hawke, banished him from the game.

George Lohmann of Surrey was an outstanding medium-pace bowler whose career ended prematurely because he played too much cricket. He made his first-class debut aged 19 in 1884, was in the Test team by 1886, but left the game a decade later with 112 wickets in 18 Tests at 10.75 each. In total he took 1,841 first-class wickets at 13.73.

As Lohmann reached the end of his time at the Oval, the first of the great English fast bowlers was emerging. Tom Richardson's first-class career spanned the years 1892 to 1905, during which he took 2,104 wickets at 18.43. He was reckoned to be as fast as

ABOVE A. C. MacLaren in 1902

THE PLAYERS

ABOVE Tom Richardson – one of the first great fast bowlers

any of his day, and so accurate that nearly half his wickets were bowled.

As Richardson was finishing, Sydney Barnes was starting his career. He could move the ball through the air both ways, bowl both varieties of cutter and spin it either way. He was simply the most complete bowler the game has seen, but he played first-class county cricket only when he felt like it. Most of his long career – he was still bowling when over 60 – was spent in the leagues and for Staffordshire, but he played in 27 Tests, taking 189 wickets at 16.43 apiece.

Gilbert Jessop was a batsman who struck fear into the heart of any bowler. In 1897 he scored 101 out of Gloucestershire's total of 118 against Yorkshire, in only 40 minutes. Against Australia at the Oval in 1902 he went in with England 48 for five on a worn pitch needing 273 to win. He scored 104 in 75 minutes.

For several years it was asked who was the best all-rounder in the land. The answer was that he bowled left arm, batted right-handed, and came from Kirkheaton in Yorkshire. That description fitted both George Hirst and Wilfred Rhodes, although Rhodes was the more successful, both as batsman and bowler. Both bowled spin, while Hirst added medium pace cutters. Rhodes played Test cricket for 31

THE PLAYERS

years, and took over 4,000 first-class wickets, to say nothing of scoring over 70,000 runs. Hirst managed only 36,356 runs and 2,742 wickets. Only!

When it comes to sporting all-rounders, none was greater than C.B. Fry. He was mainly a batsman, averaging over 50 during a first-class career that spanned 30 summers. He bowled as well, but his status as an all-rounder was not confined to cricket. While good enough to score a century for England against Australia, he also played soccer for England and in the FA Cup final, broke the world long-jump record, would have got a Blue for rugby but for injury, and was more than proficient at tennis, golf, boxing and rowing. For good measure, he also stood for parliament and was offered the throne of Albania.

Frank Woolley confined his talents to cricket, where he was an all-rounder of the highest class. He recorded some impressive statistics, but the style of his left-handed batting exuded pure charm. At over six feet tall he extracted bounce from most wickets, held some spectacular slip catches and had a career stretching from 1906 to 1938.

If Barnes was the ultimate bowler, it could be said that Jack Hobbs was the ultimate batsman. The first professional cricketer to be knighted, in 1953, his batting supremacy had

ABOVE Wilfred Rhodes

THE PLAYERS

ABOVE Sydney Barnes demonstrates his bowling action, 1920

earned him another title much earlier – 'The Master'. In his first-class career with Surrey and England he scored 61,237 runs with 197 centuries. He was 36 when cricket resumed after the Great War, yet he recorded 132 of his hundreds after 1918.

Hobbs formed a legendary opening partnership with Herbert Sutcliffe, who himself scored over 50,000 first-class runs. They opened the batting 38 times for England, and on 15 of those occasions forged a century opening stand. Sutcliffe's opening partner for Yorkshire was Percy Holmes. They shared 74 stands in excess of a hundred during their 14 years together, the most notable being the 555 they put on against Essex at Leyton in 1932.

Harold Larwood made his England debut in 1926, but in 1932/33 was propelled to fame and infamy as the spearhead, with Bill Voce, of England's Bodyline attack. Larwood was quick by any standard in any age, although in more recent times there have been questions about the legitimacy of his action. He terrorised the Australian batsmen in what was to be his final series before cricket politics took him out of Test reckoning. Larwood bagged 33 wickets in those five Tests in Australia at under 20, while his Nottinghamshire colleague Voce took 15 in four.

Wally Hammond batted with poise

and grace, particularly against spin, while in the slips he made even the most difficult catches seem almost effortless. To support his claim to be considered among the very best, consider his statistics for the 1928/29 tour to Australia. 905 runs at an average of 113.12, with 251 in the second Test at Sydney, 200 in the third at Melbourne and in the fourth, at Adelaide, he followed an unbeaten 119 with 177.

Apart from the appearance of

ABOVE Wally Hammond was captain of England in Australia 1946/47

THE PLAYERS

fearsome fast bowlers, the period up to the Second World War was marked by some outstanding spinners. Hedley Verity bowled left-arm spin until he lost his life in the conflict, while 'Tich' Freeman took over 200 wickets with his leg-breaks in eight consecutive seasons, and managed 304 in 1928. He finished with 3,776 wickets in first-class cricket and 66 in his 12 Tests.

Len Hutton set a world record for the highest individual Test innings that stood for a generation, and was knighted following retirement. His individual Test record of 364 came when he was only 22, but he maintained his career at the very highest standard. If there were doubts about appointing him as the first professional captain of England, he dispelled them. He led England to the Ashes in 1953, retained them in 1954/55 and never had a series defeat to his name in the six he was skipper.

That was despite losing the first Test on the 1954/55 tour to Australia, when he had a potent weapon at his disposal in Frank Tyson. 'The Typhoon' burst on the scene on that tour with 28 wickets at 20.82, bowling with a ferocity seldom witnessed. His action was not a

THE PLAYERS

thing of beauty and it put such a strain on his body that he played in only 17 Tests, taking 76 wickets at 18.56.

Tyson was the main destroyer of Australia on that expedition because the most acclaimed bowler was not properly fit. Alec Bedser was a shadow of the man who had taken 39 wickets in the 1953 series. A master of swing and cut, Bedser was the mainstay of the England attack throughout his career, during which he took a then record 236 wickets.

England had other great bowlers in the same era. Fred Trueman and Brian Statham formed as potent an opening attack as the country has seen. Statham quietly took wickets with his unerring accuracy, while the more flamboyant Trueman was full of showmanship and theatricals. He finished with 307 wickets, 29 of them coming when he terrorised the Indians in his debut series of 1952. Statham claimed 252 and these two fine bowlers carried the England attack for over a decade.

Trevor Bailey was a fine third seamer and a genuine all-rounder by his own definition, worth a place in the side as a bowler or as a batsman. But England also had a fine spin partnership at the time. Jim Laker (off breaks) and Tony Lock (left arm) were as good as any, with Laker himself peerless. Lock's career was overshadowed by his dubious action, but he worked hard to eradicate the imperfection. Laker

LEFT Len Hutton

BELOW Frank Tyson in action against Australia in 1954/55

ABOVE Denis Compton

needed no such remedial work. The highlight of his career came at Old Trafford in 1956 with his amazing feat of taking nine Australian wickets for 37 in the first innings, followed by all ten for 53 in the second.

Amongst England's classy batsmen at this time, Denis Compton was a genius. Although he made his Test debut in 1937 with 65 against New Zealand, his great years came after the war. In 1947 he scored 3,816 runs, including 18 centuries, two of them in the same Test against Australia. Back home he decimated South Africa with 65, 163, 208, 115, 6, 30, 53 and 113. Then, in 1953, with his "Middlesex Twin" Bill Edrich at the other end, he hit the winning runs to ensure England's Ashes triumph.

Colin Cowdrey could be compared with the best. His stroke-play was

THE PLAYERS

exquisite, with a deft touch for a big man. He played in 114 Tests, recorded 22 centuries and held 120 catches, mainly at slip. Peter May took over the England captaincy from Hutton and was rated as highly as his predecessor as a batsman and a captain. Always poised with a bat in his hand, he was the epitome of the English gentleman, yet as hard a captain as most who played under or against him ever encountered.

Tom Graveney was another stylist who made the game look ridiculously easy, while Ken Barrington made it look anything but. Nevertheless, he could grind out a big score when it mattered and he averaged 58.67 in his 82-Test career, with 20 hundreds. Keeping wicket in the same side was Godfrey Evans, a genuine wicket-keeper/batsman. He followed in the Kent and England footsteps of another great, Les Ames, and was the predecessor of yet another in Alan Knott. All three served England with distinction both in front of and behind the stumps.

Ted Dexter was to follow May as an England captain in the classical batting mould. Dexter could destroy any attack and was another multi-talented individual who could play golf to international standard, and even flew

BELOW Ted Dexter batting for Sussex against the Australians at Hove in 1964

THE PLAYERS

himself to Australia. Naturally an attacking player, he could defend when he needed to. That was something Geoff Boycott could do better than most. Labelled as a somewhat selfish player, he was an outstanding technician who was as safe a bet as any if a doughty innings was required.

Among the English bowlers to take the honours towards the end of the 20th century, John Snow and Bob Willis were among the most successful quicks, while Geoff Arnold provided Knott with more Test dismissals than anyone, even his Kent colleague Derek Underwood. The left-arm spinner, delivering rather quicker than most of his style, was only 25 when he took his one thousandth first-class wicket, finished with 2,465 and after 86 matches, he finished three short of 300 in Tests.

England relied very much on what might be termed G force for runs at this time. Nobody scored more than Graham Gooch. After a pair on his Test debut, he went on to make 8,900 in Tests and more runs in first-class and limited-overs cricket than anyone else ever to play the game. His top Test score of 333 came against India in 1990 at Lord's when he was captain, and he followed that with 123 in the second innings for a record match aggregate of 456.

David Gower was all languid grace, with some of the most handsome shots imaginable. By contrast, another captain, Mike Gatting, was full of punchy aggression. It took him 54 innings to reach a hundred in Tests, but he went on to make ten, along with 21 fifties. Controversy dogged his captaincy, but his contribution to English cricket was immense.

Tony Greig was primarily a batsman but good enough as a bowler in either medium pace or spinning roles to creep into the all-rounder category. There have been wicket-keeper/batsmen all-rounders like Knott and Alec Stewart, who played

ABOVE Graham Gooch batting during his historic innings of 333 in the first Test at Lord's against India in 1990

LEFT David Gower celebrates

THE LITTLE BOOK OF CRICKET **121**

THE PLAYERS

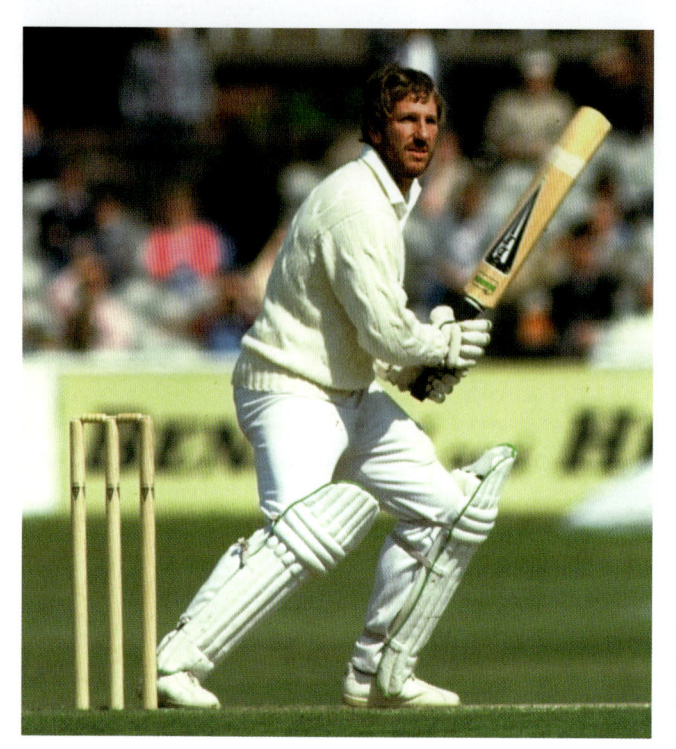

ABOVE Four more for Ian Botham during his 149 not out against Australia at Headingley in 1981

over 100 Tests, but above them all was the genuine article in Ian Botham. Botham announced himself at international level in 1977 at the age of just 21, before becoming England's match-winner.

In three Ashes Tests in 1981, immediately after resigning the captaincy when in poor personal form, he thrilled an entire nation with his all-round heroics. He scored an unbeaten 149 at Headingley, he played an innings of 118 at Old Trafford that was arguably even greater, and in between he charged in like a bull to demolish Australia's batting at Edgbaston. In all, he played in 102 Tests, scored 5,200 runs at an average of 33.54, and took 383 wickets at 28.40.

After his exploits in the Ashes series of 2005, Andrew Flintoff might well measure up to the standards of a great all-rounder, although unlike Botham he has suffered more than his share of injuries. So has the 2005 Ashes-winning captain Michael Vaughan. His outstanding time as a batsman came in the 2002/03 Ashes series when he averaged 66.30 in Australia, with three hundreds. He was rated as the world's number one batsman at the time, just as Stephen Harmison headed the bowlers' list after taking 23 wickets at

14.86 in the Caribbean in 2003/04.

The list of players from overseas is equally studded with outstanding names. While Grace marked a watershed in English cricket, Don Bradman overshadows everyone from Australia. Before his career, spanning the years 1928 to 1948, there were fast bowlers like Frederick "The Demon" Spofforth and batsmen like Victor Trumper. The Australian greats after him have been legion, with the names of Richie Benaud, Ray Lindwall, Keith Miller, Dennis Lillee, Greg Chappell, Allan Border, Steve Waugh, Shane Warne and Ricky Ponting eligible for any list of legends.

Bradman, however, has been unsurpassed as a batsman in the history of the game. Of players appearing in more than 20 Tests, the second highest average stands at 60.97. Bradman's was 99.94. He also averaged a century every three innings in first-class cricket, and held the record for the highest individual score in both first-class and Test cricket (452 not out and 334).

The second highest average belongs to Graeme Pollock of South Africa. He was amongst the last of his countrymen to have anything like a decent Test career before the Apartheid years, with contemporaries like Barry Richards and Mike Procter missing out. Since their readmission Allan Donald, Jonty Rhodes and Jacques Kallis have touched greatness.

New Zealand has produced Bert

ABOVE Andrew Flintoff captaining England against Sri Lanka in the third Test at Trent Bridge, 2006

THE PLAYERS

RIGHT Imran Khan takes the wicket of England's Richard Illingworth as Pakistan win the World Cup in 1992

Sutcliffe, Richard Hadlee and Martin Crowe amongst the greats, while one of the newer Test nations, Zimbabwe, can offer Andy Flower. From Sri Lanka, Aravinda de Silva and Sanath Jayasuriya have been dwarfed by Muttiah Muralitharan, whose dubious bowling action alone prevents him from automatic selection among the greatest of all time.

Pakistan has produced so many great players since attaining Test status in its own right in 1952. Hanif Mohammad and Fazal Mahmood starred in the early days, while Zaheer Abbas, Javed Miandad, Imran Khan, Abdul Qadir, Wasim Akram, Waqar Younis and Inzamam-ul-Haq have been worthy successors. Sunil Gavaskar was the outstanding Indian batsman between 1971 and 1987, and the all-rounder Kapil Dev took over the national mantle before Sachin Tendulkar assumed greatness as a batsman to compare with the best of any generation or nationality. Anil Kumble made his mark by becoming only the second player to take all ten wickets in a Test innings.

Perhaps no area has produced great players like the Caribbean. George Headley was the first in the 1930s, followed by the 'Three Ws' (Frank Worrell, Everton Weekes and Clyde Walcott), Lance Gibbs, Wes Hall, Clive Lloyd, Andy Roberts, Malcolm Marshall, Viv Richards, Courtney

Walsh and Brian Lara. Surpassing them all was Garry Sobers. If Grace and Bradman set the standards in their eras, Sobers could have walked into any team as a batsman alone, but he was also a top-class bowler in three styles, and he possessed a rare ability as a fielder. He was the complete all-rounder and of all the great players mentioned, and plenty more who have not been, Sobers stands out, the defining talent in his day as Grace was in his.

Available Now

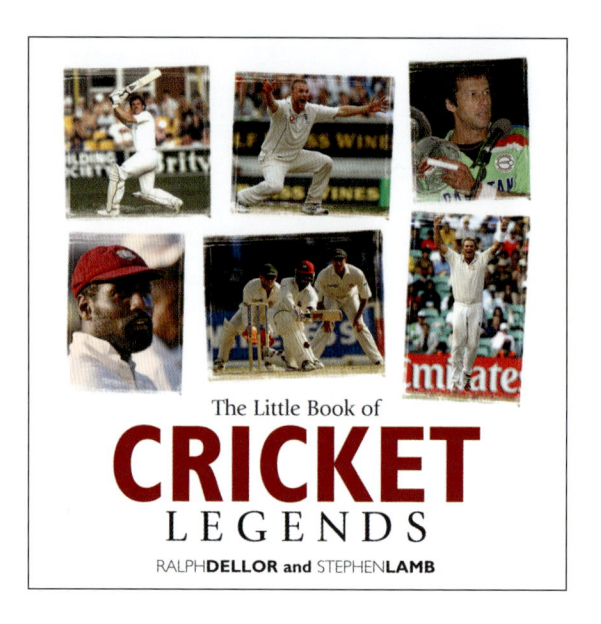

The Little Book of
CRICKET
LEGENDS
RALPH**DELLOR** and STEPHEN**LAMB**

Available from all major stockists of books or online at:
www.greenumbrellashop.co.uk

The pictures in this book were provided courtesy of the following:

GETTY IMAGES
101 Bayham Street, London NW1 0AG

Book design and artwork by Newleaf Design

Published by Green Umbrella

Publishers Jules Gammond & Vanessa Gardner

Written by Ralph Dellor and Stephen Lamb